"The race of life is not over with because we fall, nor because we are disqualified by other people. Our pain and discouragements should not be used to take us out of this race. Giving up on oneself is just one option among so many. We have to continue in the race until God says it is over. Everything we need can be found in the blood of Jesus Christ. One moment in the presence of Jesus will change your whole life. I have come to know that there is no way to be in the presence of Jesus Christ and not realize how loved, how important, and how special we are to God. To God be the glory."

—Dr. Carolyn Haney Fields
Smith

Acknowledgements

To my loving and patient husband, Kent Smith, who took care of the house, himself, and me as I wrote this book. I thank God for him.

To my editors, Susanne Lakin and Christina Miller. I cannot put into words how God blessed me when He connected me to this pair of godly women.

To all the readers of my first two books. I want to thank each of you, and I wish to thank all my new readers in advance.

To all my supporters, especially Cathy Johnson, Carol Alexander, Mrs. Nawls, and all who prayed for me. I thank you. God bless each of you.

To God be the glory.

Dedication

I dedicate this book to my Lord and Savior.

I was encouraged and inspired to write this book for several reasons. First, I write because God told me to, and I am trying to be obedient to Him. I owe my Heavenly Father so much, and there is no way I could repay Him for all He has done and is still doing for me. I hope these books will inspire others to desire to draw closer to Him. There is only one way, and that is through Jesus Christ, my Lord and Savior.

In my first book and second books, I acknowledged my personal battle with mental disorders. This is still an ongoing battle for me. There is much pain and suffering in this world and a very small amount of love, patience, compassion, and concern for others. In many instances, this may result in someone being counted out.

In this book, God allowed me to focus on those of us who allow others to count us out. But sometimes we count ourselves out. I will always want my grandchildren to know that all things are possible through Jesus Christ. I especially want this for Tyler, my first and oldest, who seems to be having a hard time finding his way. Since he is the oldest, the eyes of the whole family are on him. Maybe, in a way, we expect too much from him. In this book, I speak honestly about the pressure I may have placed on him. But my own life experiences have taught me that it is not over until God says it is.

To God be the glory!

Table of Contents

Introduction

As we look around this world today, we see a lot of uncertainty. But one thing is certain: God is still in control.

Maybe you believe, as I have heard some say, that God does not perform miracles as He did in the past. Yes, He does! God is the same in the past, the present, and the future, no matter our situation. Unbelievers and the media may say otherwise, but God is the author and finisher or our lives. God does not show favoritism or bias, and neither should you or me. Still, in today's society we like to think that all individuals are open-minded and fair. We say that we do not make personal judgments of others, but we often are responsible for mistreating others. And we are often mistreated.

Perhaps it is because of our appearance—how we dress and speak. Maybe we are too slow, too old, or too short. We lack the skills we need in order to keep up with others. Or we are too poor, came from the wrong family, have a low socioeconomic status and no education. Or perhaps our own discouragements cripple us the most. You could be among those who have allowed their spirits to be destroyed by negative words from individuals you looked up to. Your own negative thoughts about your life could be your biggest enemy.

On the other hand, you may just be a sinner needing to be saved. Some people in your world may view you as untouchable because of past immoral behavior or acts of disobedience to parents, teachers, and those in authority. Perhaps you have taken a close look at your own situation and, as a result, called it quits. For you, I say that anytime we focus too long on our problems rather than on Jesus Christ, we will likely fail.

I too was a sinner saved by the grace of God. I didn't

kill anyone in my past, although it was not from lack of trying. Nonetheless, I was still a sinner. When I learned to see myself as a sinner saved by Jesus Christ, my life changed. Now I let people identify with me by allowing them to see that, yes, I messed up. I fell down, but I keep getting up. Through Jesus Christ, our lives can change.

Although others may number us among the counted-out group, God loves us. Read what Romans 5:8 (KJV) says about the love of God: "But God commendeth his love toward us, in that, while we were yet sinners, Christ died for us."

Quick to Judge, Slow with Compassion

In an online sermon, Pastor Charlie Harris suggested that some among us have asked ourselves, "Why not me? Why doesn't anyone want me?" This may not be you, but you may have experienced the sinking feeling of insignificance and worthlessness. Even if you haven't, many in our world have, including me. Many times in our cultures and communities, individuals are counted out and overlooked, judged in many instances by their present condition or past actions and behaviors. You may take at a look at yourself and your situations and count yourself out. Sometimes we can be too hard on ourselves, trying to do things that were not in God's plan for us.

The free online dictionary that can be found on Google.com says "counted out" means to be rejected or be disqualified. Sometimes the people we love most count us out. One bad mistake can turn family members and the whole community against us. Then it's hard to see redemption for our soul, and we feel all alone.

Some among us may have made unthinkable mistakes; therefore, we now think we can't be forgiven. If we are not careful, we begin to believe we are doomed for failure. I see this happening within myself and my own family because of the expectations we place on ourselves and our loved ones. You may have had or may be dealing with this experience as you read this book.

We have all placed the burden of unrealistic expectations on ourselves and those we love. People are human. Parents, and especially you grandparents, need to know that children are human. Like us, they are not perfect. Also, Satan can use these unrealistic expectations against us when we fall. In most instances, failure, rejection, and disappointment results in discouragement. In the hands of Satan, discouragement and despair are powerful weapons. I have seen them tear families apart.

That said, many among us, including myself, may be viewed as "lowlife" individuals. In case this is unfamiliar to you, let me explain that we are the ones with no positive future and nothing worthwhile to contribute to our society. Subsequently, we are often looked over by educators, church members, wealthy politicians, those with high status, those in power or authority, and family members. Many individuals within my circle hate to hear me say the words I previous stated, but this book is about being real. So if you are among the ones counting others out, be very careful, because someone in your world has probably counted you out too. Some individuals are counted out before they are even given a chance in life.

People are counted out early in my race, particularly young African American men. I'm learning every day that past experiences or behaviors don't predict our future. If an individual of my ethnicity spends a day or night in jail, then it's over with for that person. Many of us still live with and among people with similar attitudes as the people described in John 8:4–11, as they judged the adulterous woman. And yet, read Jesus's response to their behavior:

> "Teacher, this woman was caught in the act of
> adultery. In the Law Moses commanded us to
> stone such women. Now what do you
> say?" They were using this question as a trap,
> in order to have a basis for accusing him. But
> Jesus bent down and started to write on the
> ground with his finger. When they kept on
> questioning him, he straightened up and said
> to them, "Let any one of you who is without
> sin be the first to throw a stone at her." Again
> he stooped down and wrote on the ground. At
> this, those who heard began to go away one at
> a time, the older ones first, until only Jesus
> was left, with the woman still standing
> there. Jesus straightened up and asked her,

"Woman, where are they? Has no one

condemned you?" "No one, sir," she said.

"Then neither do I condemn you," Jesus

declared. "Go now and leave your life of sin."

Yes, the above passage is about the adulterous

woman, but any sin could get the same result. Jesus Christ,

on the other hand, shows love and compassion to those of us

viewed as unequal. In Luke 7:36–48, we see a perfect

example for sinners. In it, a sinful woman anointed the feet of

our Lord and Savior. Jesus was invited to dinner at the house

of a Pharisee.

Now, the only people invited to this party were the

socially important. And yet, the Bible says a certain immoral

woman showed up. Although she was not invited, she

somehow got into this house with the invited guests. I read

nowhere that the other guests brought gifts, but she did. This immoral, ungodly woman did not come to this dinner party empty-handed. Rather, she brought a beautiful jar of expensive perfume.

If this woman had been wealthy, the price of the perfume would not have been important. Therefore, I think she was poor but willing to sacrifice so she could give her best to Jesus. Surely she knew the guests and host would reject her. And although rejection was something I believe she was used to, I don't think she could have handled it if Jesus had rejected her in front of this crowd. But thanks to Jesus, she didn't have to endure this shame.

Neither do you and I. I have read nowhere in the Bible that Jesus rejects anyone who believes in Him.

Luke does give us the name of this woman. Rather, she is introduced to us as "a sinner!" I have not found many people in the Bible who are acknowledged as she is. Because of her introduction, I believe she had a reputation. I don't know what she had done or was doing. But I do know from the Bible that Simon the Pharisee was not pleased to have her in his home. Nor was he pleased with her behavior and actions toward Jesus (Luke 7:38).

As she stood behind him at his feet weeping, she began to wet his feet with her tears. Then she wiped them with her hair, kissed them and poured perfume on them.

In verse 39, we see how Simon felt in his heart.

When the Pharisee who had invited him saw this, he said to himself, "If this man were a prophet, he would know who is touching him and what kind of woman she is—that she is a sinner."

However, Jesus knew the hearts of all men, as noted in Psalm 139:2–3 .

You know when I sit and when I rise; you perceive my thoughts from afar. You discern my going out and my lying down; you are familiar with all my ways.

Therefore, in Luke 7:40–50 , Jesus gave Simon and the crowd something to think about.

Jesus answered him, "Simon, I have something to tell you." "Tell me, teacher," he said. "Two people owed money to a certain moneylender. One owed him five hundred denarii, and the other fifty. Neither of them had the money to pay him back, so he forgave the debts of both. Now which of them will love him more?" Simon replied, "I suppose the one who had the bigger debt forgiven." "You have judged correctly," Jesus said. Then he turned toward the woman and said to Simon, "Do you see this woman? I came into your house. You did not give me any water for my feet, but she wet my feet with her tears and wiped them with her hair. You did not give me a kiss, but this woman, from the time I entered, has not stopped kissing my feet. You did not put oil on my head, but she has poured perfume on my feet. Therefore, I tell you, her many sins have been forgiven—as her great love has shown. But whoever has been forgiven little loves little." Then Jesus said to her, "Your sins are forgiven." The other guests began to say among themselves, "Who is this who even forgives sins?" Jesus said to the woman, "Your faith has saved you; go in peace."

Read through the above passage and ask yourself who you identify with in this passage. Are you the uninvited guest, alone at the end of your rope, plagued with sin and guilt and counted out by society? Or are you Simon, the self-righteous, judgmental host, thinking you are better than certain others and have the authority and right to count people in or out?

Sadly, I have been both. Neither is anything to be proud of. In both cases, I lied to myself. I was in no better shape than the ones I judged. Therefore, I also needed a savior. In truth, I was in worse shape than the uninvited guest in this passage because she had enough sense to realize she needed Jesus. I, on the other hand, had to go crazy in order to reach this realization. What about you?

Nevertheless, this uninvited dinner guest found forgiveness, love, mercy, and compassion. I found these in Jesus Christ too, so if you are not invited to the social events, parties, and big gatherings, I say to you, "It is not over until God says it is."

God Can Change You

Some of us feel we are too far gone, that God cannot reach and change us. But Jesus Christ gladly loves and accepts us. When given the opportunity, He will change our lives.

The following passage beautifully expresses Jesus's love and patience. Read John 3:1–6 and rejoice as you see how God specializes in finding and changing those we view as lost and unchangeable.

Now there was a Pharisee, a man named
Nicodemus who was a member of the Jewish
ruling council. He came to Jesus at night and
said, "Rabbi, we know that you are a teacher
who has come from God. For no one could
perform the signs you are doing if God were
not with him." Jesus replied, "Very truly I tell
you, no one can see the kingdom of God
unless they are born again." "How can
someone be born when they are old?"
Nicodemus asked. "Surely they cannot enter a
second time into their mother's womb to be
born!" Jesus answered, "Very truly I tell you,
no one can enter the kingdom of God unless
they are born of water and the Spirit. Flesh

gives birth to flesh, but the Spirit gives birth to spirit."

Let me set up the above scene for you. Nicodemus was a Pharisee and a member of the ruling council. According to the book of Matthew, the Jews had two groups of religious leaders: the Pharisees and the Sadducees. The Pharisees had separated themselves from anything they labeled non-Jewish and carefully followed the law of the Old Testament along with oral traditions handed down through the years. The Sadducees were a conservative sect that did not believe in the resurrection of the dead and only accepted the written law of Moses. Both religious groups disliked each other, and both disliked Jesus.

Nicodemus chose to come to Jesus at night, perhaps out of fear. He may have been ashamed to be seen by his peers, searching for answers and being taught by the person his group did not like. But Nicodemus was willing to come and speak personally to Jesus about his teachings. More importantly, Jesus was willing to take time to speak to him. He did not rebuke Nicodemus or call him a coward for coming to him in darkness, and he didn't refuse to talk to him. Rather, Jesus showed love, patience, and understanding toward Nicodemus and his position and role in society.

The Bible tells us very little about Nicodemus. But we can imagine that he left this meeting a changed man with a new understanding about himself and God. The new birth, which Jesus Christ spoke to him about, provides a new nature. It also gives us new principles, affections, and purpose. Here was a man who belonged to a religious sect that hated Jesus Christ. Yet the next time I read about this man is in John 7:50–52 (NLT), when he risks his reputation and position in society. At this time, he appeared as part of the Jewish high council, which met to discuss ways they could get rid of Jesus.

> Then Nicodemus, the leader who had met with
> Jesus earlier, spoke up. "Is it legal to convict a
> man before he is given a hearing?" he asked.
> They replied, "Are you from Galilee, too?
> Search the Scriptures and see for yourself—no
> prophet ever comes from Galilee!"

Yes, Nicodemus was overruled by the other leaders, but he had spoken up. He had begun to change so much that, after the death of Jesus, he and Joseph of Arimathea asked for Jesus's body so they could bury it. This act changed the secret believer into a follower of Jesus (John 19: 38–39 NLT). Don't forget this: Jesus knew how Nicodemus felt about him before they met, yet Jesus showed him that he was someone of value.

The love of God working through the Holy Spirit allows us to look at and treat other human beings with love, compassion, mercy, and hope. Jesus shows the same love through his interactions with Nicodemus. As Christians, we come from all walks of life and all kinds of backgrounds. We were shaped in iniquity, but by the grace of God, we are saved. After reading Nicodemus's story, I concluded that he received mercy, and so can we. From Genesis to Revelation, we can read about the mercy of God.

Merriam-Webster's Collegiate Dictionary, 11th Edition says mercy is a blessing that is a divine favor or compassion. God reveals His mercy toward us by not giving us what we deserve: the wrath of God (John 3:18b; 3:36b). Jesus tells us to be merciful because our God has been merciful to us (Luke 6:36).

When people are labeled, overlooked, and counted out, particularly by loved ones, they often turn from what our culture considers normal or acceptable. Some begin to see themselves as deeply different from and inferior to others. For me this is a personal issue, not just because of my background but because of the life I have today through Jesus Christ. His love and compassion allow me to see my self-worth and purpose. And as a result I can also see the self-worth of all God's children.

I pray that, as you read the words of this book, you too will see your worth and decide not to count yourself out or allow others to do so. Nor will you accept others' views about your life. Jesus Christ is in town, and he is looking for you. Be thankful that God has the last word about our lives and situations. Say these words aloud: "It is not over until God says it is."

Chapter One: The Power of Words

Bob Simon, a *60 Minutes* correspondent, once interviewed a man named Favio Chavel from a community of Cateura, Paraguay, near Asunción, the capital. In this community, garbage is a means for making money. Its citizens harvest trash twelve months a year, sifting through the rubbish for plastic and cardboard. Chavel came up with the idea of a music school for the poor children living within this poverty area. He hoped to lift them above their conditions, not realizing just how far this would take them all. From the trash he began to make violins from oven trays, cellos from oil barrels, and saxophones and trumpets from old drain pipes. The keys were once coins and bottle caps, drum skins used to be X-ray plates, and guitars were made from dessert tines.

One man's vision brought an obscure group of very

poor children into the homes of people all over the world via our televisions. This interview can still be found online. It ends with the children performing as they now do all around the world. Chavel ends the interview with Bob Simon with these words: "Send me your garbage, and we'll send it back to you as music."

Through Chavel, God changed the lives of children who, because of their situation, had been counted out by other individuals. They may have counted themselves out too. Yet long before this man existed or these children were born, God used another man, His only begotten Son, to save the whole world. John 1:1–13 says that all who welcome Jesus Christ into their lives are reborn, receiving a new life from God, his Father.

Faith in Jesus Christ brings changes in us from the inside out, rearranging our thoughts, attitudes, desires, motives, and purposes. It puts us in God's family. Chavel could offer children love, hope, dreams, possibilities, and words of encouragement, which we all need. However, God, through Jesus Christ, offers everlasting life. Satan and his followers may have seemed to win a victory at the cross of Calvary, but God turned that victory into defeat when Jesus Christ rose from the dead. Jesus overcame. We can too. We can have hope now and beyond our deaths.

First Corinthians 15:58 says that, because of the resurrection of Jesus, nothing we do for him is useless or unimportant. Chavel's vision for those children came through Jesus. Psalm 20:4 tells us "May he grant your heart's desires and make all your plans succeed" (NLT). Proverbs 16:9 says "The heart of man plans his way, but the Lord establishes his steps" (ESV). Most importantly, we can't forget Matthew 6:33 (ESV): "But seek first the kingdom of God and his righteousness, and all these things will be added to you."

If we believe in our hearts that Jesus Christ has won

the victory over this world and Satan, we should stay strong in times of discouragements and despair. As we grow through reading, praying, and meditating on the Word of God, we should begin to feel as Paul declared in Philippians 4:13: "I can do all things through Christ which strengtheneth me" (KJV). When we accept Jesus Christ and join our lives with his, we receive power through him. This enables us to do his will as well face life challenges.

But don't think for a moment that you and I are not mentally and physically affected by words from our own mouths. According to Jesus, the words we speak are the overflow of our hearts (Matthew 12:34–35 NLT). In Matthew 15:11, Jesus teaches us that what goes into our mouths doesn't defile us. We are defiled by the words that come out of our mouths.

Just think about this: we are by no means as powerful as God, but our words are not simple sounds coming out of our mouths. By the power of His words, God spoke the world into existence. There is power in the word of God. Genesis 1:26 says we are made in God's image. So criticizing ourselves and others is criticizing what God made. With our words we can destroy one's spirit and bring about hatred and violence. Words from our mouths affect other individuals, inflicting wounds as well as exacerbating suffering. Proverbs 12:6 says that our words have the power to destroy and to build up. "The words of the wicked are like a murderous ambush, but the words of the godly save lives" (NLT). In the book of James the question is asked: Do we build people up or do we tear them down? (James 4:11 NLT)

At the same time, the words of our mouths can bring about change if we express them at the right time and to the right person. One example is a blind beggar named Bartimaeus. We meet this beggar in Mark chapter 10. He is of no importance in his society because of his disability.

Bartimaeus sat beside the road as Jesus walked by. Listening to the crowd, Bartimaeus knew Jesus was near. He could hear the noise of the crowd following him.

Someone told him that Jesus of Nazareth was there. Bartimaeus then immediately shouted out, "Jesus, Son of David, have mercy on me" (Mark 10:47). The crowd said simply, "Jesus of Nazareth." Son of David is a name for the Messiah, so Bartimaeus knew who Jesus was. This blind man opened his mouth and spoke his belief that Jesus was the Messiah. His faith in Jesus resulted in his healing. Never again would Bartimaeus wear the cloak of beggar.

Many rebuked him and told him to be quiet, but he shouted all the more, "Son of David, have mercy on me!" Jesus stopped and said, "Call him." So they called to the blind man, "Cheer up! On your feet! He's calling you."

Throwing his cloak aside, he jumped to his

feet and came to Jesus. "What do you want me

to do for you?" Jesus asked him. The blind

man said, "Rabbi, I want to see." "Go," said

Jesus, "your faith has healed you."

Immediately he received his sight and

followed Jesus along the road. (Mark 10:48–

52)

Bartimaeus illustrates the importance of knowing who

Jesus Christ is and not being afraid or ashamed to

acknowledge Him, no matter the time, place, or situation. In

fact, this knowledge is power that comes from knowing who

Jesus Christ is. Jesus tells us in John 14:13 (NLT), "You can

ask for anything in my name, and I will do it, so that the Son

can bring glory to the Father." Also, Jesus tells us that all

authority in heaven and on earth has been given to him

(Matthew 28:18). When and if you come to believe the Word of Jesus, you will realize there are no disabilities that the name of Jesus cannot heal.

We see this in Acts 4:30: "Stretch out your hand to heal and perform signs and wonders through the name of your holy servant Jesus" . And in Matthew 12:31 Jesus say there is only one sin that God will not forgive, which is blasphemy against the Holy Spirit. Jesus told the religious leaders, "So I will prove to you that the Son of Man has the authority on earth to forgive sins."(Matthew 9:6 NLT).

Meanwhile, you and I must be like this beggar who refuses to allow the crowd to silence him. Before he met Jesus Christ, Bartimaeus's disability made him a social outcast, depending on others to meet his needs. According to the Bible, some people in this society viewed blindness as the result of sin (John 9:2). I see this happening to Bartimaeus.

Biblical scholars suggest that Luke also shed some light on the life of beggar in his gospel (18:35–38). He indicates that most beggars had some form of disability with no income for medical assistance because of their lack of ability to earn money. Luke goes on to add that people were more likely to ignore their obligation to care for these people. As result, beggars had little or no hope. But this beggar found hope in the same person I have: Jesus Christ. The problem people had with medical care in that day was not much different than some have today. Those who do not have to deal with medical issues may not see medical care as a major concern. But for many of us living with mental disorders, dealing daily with health-care issues can be distressing.

Early this year, I was proud to see on television that our president signed a bill that would provide more suicide prevention programs for veterans. We are a military family with many retiring veterans, so this is something I thank God for. I know the need firsthand. Then again, I must admit that while I watched this event, my heart went out to the all the other families who will live without proper mental health care because they are not veterans.

Some individuals may still hold to the same beliefs as those in Luke's day: that there is little hope for the disabled. Not true! As long as we have Jesus Christ, we have hope. A blind beggar, overlooked and seen as an outcast by his own society, knew who Jesus was. But the religious leaders, who could see Jesus performing miracles, were so blinded by sin that they could not see. Maybe 1 Corinthians 1:26–27 (NLT) will enlighten us.

> Remember, dear brothers and sisters, that few
> of you were wise in the world's eyes or
> powerful or wealthy when God called you.
> Instead, God chose things the world considers

foolish in order to shame those who think they are wise. And he chose things that are powerless to shame those who are powerful.

Bartimaeus met Jesus as beggar, and it appears to me that he was not willing to give up on God. His story ends with him as a healed follower of Jesus Christ.

I think that, for the most part, we tend to underestimate the power of our words. Look back at our history. Genocide occurred because one person said that certain other people were not worthy to live. Others were so influenced by these words that they were willing to go along with this view. On the other hand, history reveals many instances in which the words of one man or one woman have motivated positive change for many in our world. Jesus Christ is at the top of my list of influential speakers because His words offer love, forgiveness, and eternal life to all who put their faith and trust in Him.

The Greatness of God's Mercy

Many individuals in our world believe God forgives only the "little" sins, like lying, anger, drunkenness, gossiping, and bad thoughts. They don't believe He forgives sins like stealing, murder, and adultery. According to the Bible, sin is sin. All sins separate us from God, but no sin is too big for God to forgive. Although, as previously noted, there is one that God will not forgive. Whoever blasphemes against the Holy Spirit will never be for forgiven. It is an eternal sin (Mark 3:29). Everyone has sinned and no one is good enough to get into to heaven on their own (Romans 3:12). We don't get into heaven because we are good or because we work hard. Salvation is based on the grace of God. No good works and no amount of money can earn us the favor or God or get us to heaven (Ephesians 2:8–9).

When Jesus died on the cross, He paid the penalty for all the sin of the entire world (1 John 2:2).This includes past, present, and future—big and small sins—for those of us who have placed our faith in Jesus Christ. But if we don't believe in Jesus Christ, then our sins will not be forgiven. John 3:18 says, "Whoever believes in him is not condemned, but whoever does not believe stands condemned already because they have not believed in the name of God's one and only Son."

But all who believe in Jesus Christ for salvation are forgiven, no matter what sins he/she has committed (Romans 6:23; John 3:16). The Bible says that God does not show favoritism (Romans 2:11). The Bible also teaches that Christians are not to show favoritism. James highlights this in James 2:1–5:

My brothers, as believers in our glorious Lord

Jesus Christ, don't show favoritism. Suppose

a man comes into your meeting wearing a

gold ring and fine clothes, and a poor man in

shabby clothes also comes in. If you show

special attention to the man wearing fine

clothes and say, "Here's a good seat for you,"

but say to the poor man, "You stand there" or

"Sit on the floor by my feet,"

have you not discriminated among yourselves

and become judges with evil thoughts? Listen,

my dear brothers: Has not God chosen those

who are poor in the eyes of the world to be

rich in faith and to inherit the kingdom he

promised those who love him?

James is telling us that it is wrong to treat people differently based on their financial status, education, position in society, name, or appearance. Yet, as we look around our world, we can plainly see that many of us deal with this issue daily, just as they did in Bible days. I see this happening on my job and in our churches.

From my own life experiences, I now know that our start in life matters little. More important is the way we finish our journey here on earth. Our victory requires endurance and lifetime commitment to Jesus. We must keep running this race of life despite our situation and others' attitudes toward us.

Some of us have fallen behind in this race, perhaps due to illness, sin, or discouragement. When that is the case, we must get up and look up. We can't see Jesus when we look down. If you are still breathing, you have time to finish this race.

Believe me, I know from experience that sometimes it appears that all hope is gone, especially when others finish the race without us. But I'm also learning every day that it is not over until God says it is. When I heard that testimony for the first time, I didn't understand its importance. But God has brought me a long way, so now I understand. You and I are important to God. Through Him, we have value and self-worth. He is the only one who knows our beginning and our end, as we see in Isaiah 46:9–10.

> "Remember the former things, those of long ago; I am God, and there is no other; I am God, and there is none like me. I make known the end from the beginning, from ancient times, what is still to come. I say, 'My purpose will stand, and I will do all that I please.'"

I say to you the same words that the Holy Spirit speaks to me daily, and I repeat them out loud: "I can't quit and I cannot give up. Because of who I am to God, I will see God's promises for my life." Perhaps things didn't work out exactly the way we planned for our lives and the lives of our loved ones, but that doesn't mean God is not working in us. First Corinthians 10:13 (KJV) tells us this:

> There hath no temptation taken you but such as is common to man: but God is faithful, who will not suffer you to be tempted above that ye are able; but will with the temptation also make a way to escape, that ye may be able to bear it.

According to a sermon of the late and great G. E.

Patterson, the fundamental point in the above passage is that we may be able to bear it. I can't speak for you, but I want to escape hardship, disappointment, pain, rejection, and depression. But I am learning that escaping my problems may not be to my advantage. I need to know that, during these tiresome times, God has the power to keep me just as He kept Daniel.

Daniel: Counted Out by His Enemies

The entire book of Daniel is both important and encouraging. In it, we learn how the young Daniel was taken from his family and relocated to a foreign land. There he was surrounded by idolaters and enemies. Despite his environment and circumstances, Daniel showed us that faithfulness to God is more important than faithfulness to ourselves or others, even those in powerful positions. First

Samuel 15:22 teaches us that obedience to God is better than sacrifice.

Let's look for a moment at Daniel chapter 6. King Darius had just made a decree commanding the people to pray only to him for thirty days. If anyone did otherwise, they would be thrown to the lions.

> But when Daniel learned that the law had been signed, he went home and knelt down as usual in his upstairs room, with its windows open toward Jerusalem. He prayed three times a day, just as he had always done, giving thanks to his God. Then the officials went together to Daniel's house and found him praying and asking for God's help. So they went straight to the king and reminded him about his law. "Did you not sign a law that for the next thirty

days any person who prays to anyone, divine or human—except to you, Your Majesty—will be thrown into the den of lions?" "Yes," the king replied, "that decision stands; it is an official law of the Medes and Persians that cannot be revoked." (Daniel 6:10–12 NLT)

Remember that Daniel was alone. Yes, others had been taken with him to Babylon, including his three young friends. But he had no father or mother to love, comfort, encourage, or advise him. On the other hand, someone had taught this young man about God. One key part of being good parents is to teach our children the truth of God's commandments: "Impress them on your children. Talk about them when you sit at home and when you walk along the road, when you lie down and when you get up" (Deuteronomy 6:7).

The above passage emphasizes the continuing need of such instruction. We should do it at all times: at home, on the road, at night, and in the morning. Biblical truth should be the foundation of our homes. By following this commandment, we teach our children that worshiping God is an ongoing activity—not just reserved for Sunday school or Bible study. Yes, our children learn a great deal through direct teaching, but they learn much more by watching us. This is why we must be careful in everything we do and say.

Through Daniel's story, we see the importance of our actions as parents and the rewards of our work. Daniel's faith likely started with his parents. The behaviors he witnessed in his home prepared him for these hard times. How much are we preparing our children for the time we will no longer be there, whether by choice, death, or a life situation such as Daniel's?

Daniel held on to his faith by choosing to keep his prayer line open to God, as he had in the past. He knew that disobeying the king meant losing his life, but he refused to disobey God. Daniel had enough knowledge and faith in God to realize that God was the only One who could protect and keep him during challenging times. King Darius, forced to keep his word regarding his ruling, had Daniel arrested and thrown into the den of lions. Under normal conditions, Daniel would have been torn to pieces. However, there was nothing normal about what happened.

> The king said to him, "May your God, whom you serve so faithfully, rescue you." A stone was brought and placed over the mouth of the den. The king sealed the stone with his own royal seal and the seals of his nobles, so that no one could rescue Daniel. Then the king

returned to his palace and spent the night fasting. He refused his usual entertainment and couldn't sleep at all that night. Very early the next morning, the king got up and hurried out to the lions' den. When he got there, he called out in anguish, "Daniel, servant of the living God! Was your God, whom you serve so faithfully, able to rescue you from the lions?" Daniel answered, "Long live the king! My God sent his angel to shut the lions' mouths so that they would not hurt me, for I have been found innocent in his sight. And I have not wronged you, Your Majesty." The king was overjoyed and ordered that Daniel be lifted from the den. Not a scratch was found on him, for he had trusted in his God. (Daniel 6:16–23 NLT)

Amazingly, God kept Daniel safe all that night. Then, the next morning, He brought him out of this lion's den. This proves to me that even when people plot against you or you are in a dangerous situation, God can and will keep you safe and bring you through. This is just one reason you and I cannot give up or give in to the pressures of this life. God has power that no man can know or imagine.

If you continue reading this story, you will discover that the plans his enemies had plotted against Daniel ended up being their downfall. King Darius ordered the men who conspired against Daniel, along with their wives and children, to be executed by the same lions Daniel had spent the night with. Therefore, the evilness of these men of power impacted not only their lives but those of their entire families. And through Daniel's faithfulness to God, King Darius came to know God.

Then King Darius sent this message to the people of every race and nation and language throughout the world: "Peace and prosperity to you! I decree that everyone throughout my kingdom should tremble with fear before the God of Daniel. For he is the living God, and he will endure forever. His kingdom will never be destroyed, and his rule will never end. He rescues and saves his people;
he performs miraculous signs and wonders in the heavens and on earth.
He has rescued Daniel from the power of the lions." So Daniel prospered during the reign of Darius and the reign of Cyrus the Persian.
(Daniel 6:25–28 NLT)

When and if you find yourself in a foreign land (any place or situation that removes us from our comfort, security, and familiarity), think about Daniel. Such faith as Daniel had will enable us to withstand even the greatest pressure. Daniel did not give up on God, and God did not give up on him. In fact, God had the last word about Daniel's life, just as He has for us. He proves this once again in Deuteronomy 33:26–27 (NLT):

> "There is no one like the God of Israel. He rides across the heavens to help you, across the skies in majestic splendor. The eternal God is your refuge, and his everlasting arms are under you. He drives out the enemy before you; he cries out, 'Destroy them!'"

Chapter Two: The Love of God

When I think of the love of God, John 3:16 often comes to my mind: "For God loved the world so much that he gave his one and only Son, so that everyone who believes in him will not perish but have eternal life" (NLT footnote: alternate translation).

As I was writing this book one morning and thinking about all the things going on in my family, the Holy Spirit took me to the book of Hosea. Now, I am somewhat familiar with this book, especially a passage about the importance of knowledge, which helps to empower me in my own illness. I am learning daily how important it is to gain the knowledge to remain as healthy as possible, which for me includes a healthy diet of Jesus Christ.

But some people feel unfit or unqualified for the love of God. Well, according to the Word of God, we are all in the same boat. But God still loves us. So I wanted to know how the book of Hosea could make this clearer.

The Holy Spirit spoke to my spirit: "You see, the love of God is somewhat like a parent; in fact, you often compare His love to that of a mother."

This is true, although not of my own mother. Rather, it is true of my love for my children and of mothers who love their children. Some people may have a problem accepting God in this manner, and some have a problem accepting Him in any manner. But take a look Hosea and allow the Holy Spirit to show you as He showed me the love of God in a different way.

Still speaking to me, the Holy Spirit said, "Almost everyone who will read or hear about this book has at some time been in love." I had to agree; I have. So He had my attention.

"What does anyone want from the person they are in

love with?" He asked.

Still I said nothing.

"Well," the Holy Spirit (God) said, "they want to be loved in return. They want to receive the same level of commitment that they are giving."

Then He asked me, "Does this sound like what you want from Kent?"

This time I answer back by saying yes. In my heart, this was a true assumption.

Then the Holy Spirit said to me, "In the book of Hosea, you see the pure and unquestionable love of God toward a group of people who did not love Him in return."

This would be hurtful to anyone. Do you agree? I do, and I believe most of you would too.

Like a loving parent, God punishes us for our sins, but He never stops loving and pleading for our love. God's gifts to us are the same as they were in the days of Hosea:

love and compassion. Through no worthiness of our own, God forgave us, making all things right with Him. Yet, in Hosea, God uses the illustration of marriage to show His love for sinful people.

God instructed Hosea to marry a woman named Gomer. Before the wedding, God told Hosea that his wife would cause him great pain. She would leave him and cheat on him with other men. God also told him that some of Gomer's children would not be Hosea's.

Hosea is a love story about real-life events that many of us have lived. And if we haven't experienced these types of painful experiences, we probably know someone who has. The pain of their suffering is almost unbearable. For me, it was my son. He loved and married someone who cared for him but did not love him.

At one time I had eight brothers. Knowing them as I do, I can't say the words that would come out their mouths if they were given these instructions. They most likely would have been like Jonah, catching a ride in another direction. But not Hosea. He was obedient to the orders given to him by God, and he married Gomer.

Lessons from the Book of Hosea

The book of Hosea shows God's constant and persistent love for His children. Like Gomer, the children of God are quick to be unfaithful. Yet, despite our unfaithfulness, God's commitment to us never changes.

Hosea's message was for the children of Israel, but today, believers all over the world are God's chosen children. Like a parent, He waits for disobedient children to come to their senses and return home. God is still faithful and merciful. His arms still reach out to those who want to come.

In this story, Gomer, like many of us, went out into

the world and found out that the person she left Hosea for didn't care about her. So after struggling out in the world by herself, she went back to her husband. Likewise, we often call out to God when we are pain or trouble, but we do not want God to change our behaviors.

Reading the book of Hosea, I wanted to see Gomez come back out of love. But we often run to God only when things get tough and the problems get too hard to deal with. It may seem strange to think that God has feelings, but he does. I know He accepts us back at any moment after we ask Him for forgiveness of our sins. But God wants more: our love and gratitude. He wants our hearts. Reading the story of Hosea and Gomer, we may think the man had good reason for divorcing Gomer. But God said no. Hosea was to buy her back and love her.

Then the Lord said to me, "Go and love your wife again, even though she commits adultery with another lover. This will illustrate that the Lord still loves Israel, even though the people have turned to other gods and love to worship them." So I bought her back for fifteen pieces of silver and five bushels of barley and a measure of wine. (Hosea 3:1–2 NLT)

Does buying Gomer back, despite her sins, sound familiar? According to biblical scholars, while Gomer was on her own and needing support, she somehow ended up in slavery or got involved with someone who offered to give her back for a price. Either way, Hosea had to pay if he wanted her returned to him. Judging by the price, she wasn't worth much to whomever was selling her. But to Hosea, Gomer was worth the price. He loved her just as God loves us. No matter how low we sink or how far we think we are from God, He is willing to buy us back. In fact, He has already purchased up for a price: the blood of His only-begotten Son.

If Hosea and Gomer lived in my society today, Gomer would be labeled as unfit. People would tell Hosea to get rid of her. Just like many of us today, the people in that time were quick to talk about Gomer's sins.

It was easy for me to focus on the sins of my son's wife. But because of my illnesses and a growing knowledge of God, I also could see and acknowledge my son's sins and guilt too. Accepting this truth allowed me to treat my daughter-in-law with the same love, compassion, and understanding as I did my son.

I can take no credit for this mind-set. The Holy Spirit told me up front that if I cannot forgive her, I will not be forgiven. This was all I needed to hear! This young lady is the mother of my grandchildren. Although she is not my daughter-in-law, she will always be a major part of my life. Because of my behavior toward her, to this day she still introduces me as her mother-in-law.

That said, read this passage from Hosea chapter 4 and listen to God's words to the people who condemned Gomer for her sins but saw nothing wrong with their behaviors:

"You make vows and break them; you kill and steal and commit adultery. There is violence everywhere—one murder after another. That is why your land is in mourning, and everyone is wasting away. Even the wild animals, the birds of the sky, and the fish of the sea are disappearing. Don't point you finger at someone else and try to pass the blame! My complaint, you priests, is with you." (Hosea 4:2–4 NLT)

It is easy to read our Bible or hear a sermon and think of someone else who needs this message. In reality, the person reading the message or hearing the sermon is the person who needs it. Applying the Word of God to our life may help those we find fault in. If you have never read the book Hosea or if, like me, you read it in the past, I suggest reading it again. In this book, I saw the love of God for me through Hosea.

I was cheated on by a spouse, and it was a very painful thing to deal with. Also, I can see how nonbelievers and believers might have two different perspectives of this story. But through the lens of the Holy Spirit, I now see the whole concept of commitment to marriage and how it can parallel my commitment to God.

God does not overlook us, and He does not cast us out. He does, however, punish sins. Still, when we feel weak and unloved or are unable to think rationally and are weighted down with trials and tribulations, we should remember God's continual love.

God loves us, and His compassion never fails. When things are so bad that we cannot see our way, God's compassion does not stop. We see His forgiveness in the book of Hosea. We are wrong when we forget how much God loves us or when we think our sins are hopeless. Forgiveness and commitment are central in the story of Hosea. When God deals with our sins, He forgives us and shows mercy to us, but He judges our sins.

> "O Israel, stay away from idols! I am the one who answers your prayers and cares for you. I am like a tree that is always green; all your fruit comes from me." Let those who are wise understand these things. Let those with

discernment listen carefully. The paths of the Lord are true and right, and righteous people live by walking in them. But in those paths sinners stumble and fall. (Hosea 14:8–9 NLT)

When we, like Gomer, have been cast aside and have given up on ourselves, God is just as committed to us as He was on day one. God uses the commitment of marriage as an illustration of His commitment to us. We should commit to Him in the same way.

Reading Hosea brought to mind my own marriage. I now realize that when people say they've been married for many years, it was not without trials or tribulation. Having the mind-set of God keeps their focus away from their disagreements and differences. Instead, they emphasize their commitment to each other and God.

Giving up may seem easier than fighting for the things we desire, but allowing God to keep us in our situation will relieve our burden.

Marriage is all about love, commitment, forgiveness, and faithfulness. The pain of Gomer's betrayal of Hosea reflects a clear manifestation of God's love. Like Gomer, you and I have betrayed the One who gives us life and loves us as no one else does. No one in this story loved Gomer like Hosea did. Through Hosea, she had self-worth. Likewise, through God, I know that I am important. So are you.

However, adultery is a sin. It separated Hosea from Gomer. Sins do the same thing to our relationship with God, bringing separation. God hates sin simply because it separates us from Him: "But your iniquities have separated you from your God; your sins have hidden his face from you, so that he will not hear" (Isaiah 59:2). "I will punish the world for its evil, the wicked for their sins. I will put an end to the arrogance of the haughty and will humble the pride of the ruthless" (Isaiah 13:11). "Your wrongdoings have kept these away; your sins have deprived you of good" (Jeremiah 5:25).

It is God's will for us to have personal and eternal relationships with Him through salvation (John 3:13–16). Still, trusting God is vital to keeping our commitments to Him, to others, and to ourselves. So don't let anyone try to talk you into giving up on yourself, your spouse, your children, your grandchildren, or other family members. Nancy Missler, author and founder of The King's High Way Ministries, says that trusting God means cleaving to Him with unreserved confidence no matter how we feel, what we see, or what we understand, being fully persuaded that what He has promised, He will perform in His timing and His way. We must unconditionally believe that, through Jesus, God will accomplish all He intended for us. Tell God about your situation and listen to what He has to say. Then do as He says.

You may read this book and think, "Well, in her first book she said that she gave up on her first husband." This is true. I don't remember talking to God about the many situations I dealt with in my first marriage. So I will never know what God would have told me about my marriage. Maybe if I had talked to Him, I would not have ended up in a mental hospital. Who knows? Only God! From studying the book of Hosea, I know that my commitment to God and my commitment to my present husband are interconnected. I cannot change the past, but I can honor God and my husband.

Reading Hosea, I also realized the faithfulness of my husband. The Holy Spirit guided my mind back down the road of my marriage. Many times I didn't know who my husband was or what role he played in my life. In fact, he has been by my side during some of the lowest and darkest days of my life as I learned to live with my mental disorders. Yet I now know that God did not allow him to put me away for good or to leave me for others to care for. For many years, my husband was my voice, my eyes, and my ears. He was committed and faithful to my needs as well as the needs of our home. God took a man who had been raised to believe that the duties of the home were women's work and turned him into a man who understood that patience, mercy, and compassion were more important than traditions.

Kent was and still is faithful, caring, compassionate, and mindful of my feelings about my limitations. I realize now that my illness caused him to suffer too, like Hosea's longsuffering with Gomer. Kent's faithfulness to God inspired him to fight for me and this marriage. For that I'm truly thankful. I also thank God for the story of Hosea and Gomer, for through them I saw the working of God in my own marriage and the working of the Holy Spirit in both our lives.

Leviticus 20:10 says that both the adulterer and the adulteress are to be put to death. But in Hosea, Gomer found longsuffering, forgiveness, mercy, and compassion for her sins. God, too, forgives us for our sins. Marriages can be saved, relationships can be put back together, we can be healed from pain and disappointment, and commitments can be honored. And through the love of God, we can all have His saving grace.

There is hope for anyone who reaches out to God. No one has the last word about your life or your marriage except the Maker and Creator of your life, who is God. As Hosea went after Gomer and brought her back to him, God also pursues us in our sin. When I would not reach out to God, He came after me. Like Gomer, I did not deserve unchanging and everlasting love. The book of Hosea is a perfect example of the love of God to all of us who left Him for other gods. It shows what forgiveness and restoration look like in a close relationship. God also uses the book of Hosea to show us that no one sits outside God's offer of forgiveness. This is good news, people.

Rebirth through Jesus Christ

People in your life may not be able to see God's plans for you. Maybe you can't either. Hence, they may count you out of the race. But to be honest, sometimes we count ourselves out. If truth be told, it's easier to quit than to fight and stay in the race. And since we can see only our current situation or our beginnings rather than our ending, we give up. This is another reason reading and studying the Word of God is essential to my survival, and maybe to yours. There is hope in the Word of God!

Read Ezekiel 37:1–14 below. Listen to the dialogue between the prophet Ezekiel and God regarding a valley of dry bones covering the floor of the valley:

The hand of the Lord was on me, and he brought me out by the Spirit of the Lord and set me in the middle of a valley; it was full of bones. He led me back and forth among them, and I saw a great many bones on the floor of the valley, bones that were very dry. He asked me, "Son of man, can these bones live?" I said, "Sovereign Lord, you alone know." Then he said to me, "Prophesy to these bones and say to them, 'Dry bones, hear the word of the Lord! This is what the Sovereign Lord says to these bones: I will make breath enter you, and you will come to life. I will attach tendons to

you and make flesh come upon you and cover
you with skin; I will put breath in you, and
you will come to life. Then you will know that
I am the Lord.'" So I prophesied as I was
commanded. And as I was prophesying, there
was a noise, a rattling sound, and the bones
came together, bone to bone. I looked, and
tendons and flesh appeared on them and skin
covered them, but there was no breath in
them. Then he said to me, "Prophesy to the
breath; prophesy, son of man, and say to it,
'This is what the Sovereign Lord says: Come,
breath, from the four winds and breathe into
these slain, that they may live.'" So I
prophesied as he commanded me, and breath
entered them; they came to life and stood up
on their feet—a vast army. Then he said to

me: "Son of man, these bones are the people

of Israel. They say, 'Our bones are dried up

and our hope is gone; we are cut

off.' Therefore prophesy and say to them:

'This is what the Sovereign Lord says: My

people, I am going to open your graves and

bring you up from them; I will bring you back

to the land of Israel. Then you, my people,

will know that I am the Lord, when I open

your graves and bring you up from them. I

will put my Spirit in you and you will live,

and I will settle you in your own land. Then

you will know that I the Lord have spoken,

and I have done it, declares the Lord.'"

Doesn't it give you great assurance when you finally

realize that our lives depend on the power of God and not on our strengths, abilities, or circumstances? You may see it differently, but for me the above passage is a symbol of people whose hope has died and had been dead for a long time. In fact, biblical scholars indicate that the above passage is a picture of Jews in captivity, scattered, and dead. This particular situation Ezekiel witnessed may have appeared hopeless, with no future for reestablishing any kind of life, just graves full of dry bones. But God, the only restorer, asked Ezekiel a question I have asked myself many times. You may have too, since we sometimes cannot see past our situations. He asked, "Son of man, can these bones become living people again?" (Ezekiel 37:3 NLT) Because of Ezekiel's experience with the people of God, he felt as many of us have and still do: that there was no possibility for life in these dry bones. Nevertheless, Ezekiel did the right thing by admitting he did not know. He could see not a human solution, which is something that happens in all our lives at one time or another.

This may be why many people are quick to give up on themselves and others. Still, Ezekiel did something that most of us fail to do: put forward a perfect example. He admitted that God alone knew the answer to His question. Due to our situations, failures, socioeconomic status, or disabilities, we may look as if we have lost the race, and man has counted us out. Satan may tell you, as he has told me many times, "It's over. Just give up. You will never make it. You've lost."

During these times, God allows my mind to go back to a sermon preached by the late G. E. Patterson. He said our turnarounds come into view when we listen to the Word of God and focus our eyes on Jesus Christ.

Romans 10:17 (KJV) tell us, "So then faith cometh by hearing, and hearing by the word of God." Words have power. As God told Ezekiel to speak to the dry bones, we need to allow the Holy Spirit to speak the Word of God into our hearts. "It is the spirit that quickeneth; the flesh profiteth nothing: the words that I speak unto you, they are spirit, and they are life" (John 6:63 KJV). The Bible gives us many instances of the power of the Word of God, but for this section I will highlight only a few.

Take a look with me at Mark 5:21–43 (NLT). In this book, a crowd followed Jesus, and some within the crowd needed help. The Bible points out two of those individuals who desperately needed to get to Jesus. First, Jairus needed a healing for his dying twelve-year-old daughter. Any parent or grandparent reading his story can understand his fear for her life. The Bible says that Jairus, a leader of the local synagogue, displayed great respect by falling and kneeing before Jesus, pleading fervently with him. "'My little daughter is dying,' he said. 'Please come and lay your hands on her; heal her so she can live'" (verse 23).

At the same time, a woman pushed her way through the crowd, toward Jesus. This woman had been sick for twelve years, and her sickness was a private, personal one. Bible scholars say she had an incurable condition that caused her to bleed constantly. In that case, society would have deemed her unclean. Therefore, it would have been unlawful for her even to be in a crowd.

Leviticus 15:25–27 addresses women with a discharge of blood for many days at a time, other than a monthly period, or has a discharge that continues beyond a normal period. It states that she will be unclean as long as she has the discharge, just as in the days of her period. Any bed she lies on while her discharge continues will be unclean, as is her bed during her monthly period. Everything she sits on will be unclean, as during her period. Anyone who touches her will be unclean, including her own family members, who must wash their clothes and bathe with water, and they would remain unclean till evening. This, therefore, was not a disease she would have felt comfortable speaking about in a large crowd. It would have excluded her from most social contact.

To this day, I don't feel comfortable talking about my mental disorders to some individuals. According to the Bible, this woman had suffered a great deal from many doctors and had spent a lot of money paying them, and she had gotten not better but worse (Mark 5:26). This woman must have heard of Jesus and how he had performed miracles. I don't know what the woman knew, but one thing seems clear: she was willing to break the law for a healing.

She believed that if she could just touch the fringe of Jesus's robe, she would be healed. Get this: she wasn't trying to touch Jesus or get him to lay hands on her. The woman simply wanted to touch his robe.

What does this tell you about her faith and yours? Her faith was so strong, she knew all she had to do was touch anything Jesus had on. She needed something only Jesus could perform—a miracle. So she went to the one who could heal her. G. E. Patterson pointed out that, among all the people in this crowd who may have gotten as close to Jesus as she did, she was the only one the Bible says was healed at this particular time and place.

Her name may not be important, but the lesson I learned from her encounter with my Lord and Savior is priceless. Banned from society and human contact, she did not let others determine her faith.

Chapter Three: Healing through Jesus

Just like today, many individuals followed Jesus for many reasons. The woman with the blood problem had somehow heard about Jesus, and she believed in His ability to perform miracles. As a result, her faith is illustrated through her willingness to settle for a piece of Jesus's robe.

This woman may have felt as I have. Living with a socially unacceptable disease, she may have felt undeserving of Jesus's hands. But, oh, how wrong she was. Jesus offered up his entire body out of love for her and us. Reaching out to Jesus in faith in the midst of this crowd took courage. That meant she had to let go of whatever fear she had and be healed.

And more importantly, Jesus's reaction was as immediate as her healing. The Bible says, "Jesus realized at once that healing power had gone out from him, so he turned

around in the crown and asked, 'Who touched my robe?'"
(Mark 5:30 NLT). Jesus knew who the person was who
touched him, but he wants us to know that genuine faith
involves action.

Saying you have faith in God is one thing. Acting on
this faith shows how strong your faith really is. According to
the Bible, God gives us all a measure of faith (Roman 12:3).
But faith also includes trust. The woman in the above story
trusted in Jesus enough to risk her life and enter this
unfriendly crowd. For that, Jesus told her, "Daughter, your
faith has made you well" (Mark 5:34 NLT).

I try to live my daily life by this example, despite how
I feel. Sometimes I have felt as if my mental disorders keep
me from God as it has people in my life. But this story shows
me God's love and compassion and that He is always ready
to help. We should never allow fear to keep us from reaching
out to God. And just as important, we must trust that Jesus

can do more than one thing at a time. We can see this in the next passage. While Jesus was still dealing with the aftereffects the healing of this woman, this happened:

> While Jesus was still speaking, some people came from the house of Jairus, the synagogue leader. "Your daughter is dead," they said. "Why bother the teacher anymore?" Overhearing what they said, Jesus told him, "Don't be afraid; just believe." He did not let anyone follow him except Peter, James and John the brother of James. When they came to the home of the synagogue leader, Jesus saw a commotion, with people crying and wailing loudly. He went in and said to them, "Why all this commotion and wailing? The child is not dead but asleep." But

they laughed at him. After he put them all out, he took the child's father and mother and the disciples who were with him, and went in where the child was. He took her by the hand and said to her, *"Talitha koum!"* (which means "Little girl, I say to you, get up!") Immediately the girl stood up and began to walk around (she was twelve years old). At this they were completely astonished. He gave strict orders not to let anyone know about this, and told them to give her something to eat. (Mark 5:35–43)

Let's look closely at a couple more people who seemed without hope. First, Jesus's friend Lazarus got sick and died before Jesus came to Bethany. Getting word of his sickness but not yet his death, Jesus stated that the sickness was not unto death but for the glory of God, that the Son of God may be glorified through it. Although Jesus loved His friend and his sisters, he stayed two more days in the place where he was (John 11:4–6).

Lazarus was not just dead but had been dead four days. This meant his body had begun to decay. To me, a man dead four days is similar to the dry bones Ezekiel dealt with. It is humanly impossible for a man dead four days to live again. But it was not impossible for Jesus, who has power over life and death. So Jesus offered hope to Lazarus's sister, telling her that her brother would rise again. Martha responded with belief, agreeing that Lazarus would rise when everyone else did on Resurrection Day. Then Jesus told her, "I'm the resurrection and the life" (John 11:24–25).

Then Jesus said, "Did I not tell you that if you believe, you will see the glory of God?" So they took away the stone. Then Jesus looked up and said, "Father, I thank you that you have heard me. I knew that you always hear me, but I said this for the benefit of the people standing here, that they may believe that you sent me." When he had said this, Jesus called in a loud voice, "Lazarus, come out!" The dead man came out, his hands and feet wrapped with strips of linen, and a cloth around his face. Jesus said to them, "Take off the grave clothes and let him go." (John 11:40–44)

In this story, the sister may have believed that, since they were Jesus's friends, he would come as soon as he heard about the condition of his dear friend Lazarus. However, in this story we see that God does not always come or answer our cry for help when we want. During this time, our faith is put to an important test. I'm learning that when it is humanly impossible for me to solve my situation, God steps in. For this reason, no one can doubt that God was the one to solve my problems.

Let's look now at Luke 7:11–1. One day, when Jesus and his disciples entered a gate leading to the village of Nain, a large crowd followed, as always, He came upon a funeral procession, and the dead person was the only son of the widow. This widow was not alone; many mourners came with her from the village. In my experience with the death of loved ones, after the funeral is over, most of the people leave the bereaved alone. This mother was a widow, which means she had already experienced the loss of her husband. From studying the Bible, I can assume that, with the death of her son, she would be alone and without income or support. She had nothing to help her survive in this world. Unlike us, she had no Social Security.

In Exodus 22:22–23 (NLT), God says, "If you exploit them [widows] in any way and they cry out to me, then I will certainly hear their cry." In 1 Timothy, Paul provides more detailed instructions on caring for and supporting widows: "But if she has children or grandchildren, their first responsibility is to show godliness at home and repay their parents by taking care of them. This is something that pleases God" (1 Timothy 5:4 NLT). Paul also instructs that, in order for a widow to be supported by the church, she must be over the age of sixty. She must also have been faithful to her husband and have led a godly life. And she must have no family member to care for her (1 Timothy 5:9–10 NLT).

So for this widow, the death of her son was a serious situation. She may have seen no way to survive because, most likely, the mourners would not be there later to care for her or her needs.

Luke's gospel repeatedly emphasizes the fact that the widow was the kind of person Jesus came into this world to help. And he did just that. Through Jesus, hope can come out of any tragedy. Think about it. This woman's son was dead! Some of you may not have experienced a loss like this firsthand. Luke tells us that when Jesus saw this widow, "His heart overflowed with compassion. 'Don't cry!' he said. Then he walked over to the coffin and touched it, and the bearers stopped. 'Young man,' he said, 'I tell you, get up.' Then the dead boy sat up and began to talk! And Jesus gave him back to his mother" (Luke 7:13–15 NLT). This is a fulfillment of God's promise to help widows who cried out to Him for help.

This story is a demonstration of our salvation. We, like the dead boy, were dead in our sin. Just like the widow and her son, we were unable to help ourselves because we were in the same shape as they. But God had compassion on us and sent Jesus to raise us to life with Him. Also, like the dead son, none of us can earn a second chance at life, but we can accept the gift of life God offers. Thank God for it, and use your life to bring Him glory. (Ephesians 2:1–7)

Counted In through Jesus

My conclusion from these stories is that Jesus's disciples, his friends Mary and Martha, the onlookers, and the mourners may have believed it was all over for Jairus's daughter, Lazarus, and the widow's son.

I don't group the woman with the blood illness with the other individuals needing help from Jesus. Because of the issues concerning her illness, she was already deemed unfit by her society. So she had long been counted out. I, however, refuse to put her in the group of individuals who count themselves out, because she displayed willingness to do something about her situation. What about you?

Despite the onlookers' disbelief, Jesus brought Jairus's daughter back to life in front of her parents and three of his disciples (Luke 8:51)—after he had healed the woman who was not afraid to fight a crowd in order to touch him. Jesus also brought life back to Lazarus and the widow's son, highlighting his authority and his power to give life, physical and spiritual, to all who believe in him.

Each of the above stories shows me that God had said it was not over for these individuals. I came to the same conclusion when I studied John's account of the paralyzed man at the pool of Bethesda. He'd been sick for thirty-eight years—a long time to be sick and helpless. When the water was stirred up, whoever entered first was the one who was healed. The others had to wait for another stirring of the water. But because of his illness, this man could not move fast enough to be first into the pool.

This could have been a hopeless situation because of the lack of help from others and his inability to help himself. We, like the lame man, can allow ourselves to be trapped in our infirmities and bound by tradition. This feeling of helplessness I know from my own illnesses. I have help in my situation, but it seems this man had no one to help him.

I believe that the paralyzed man wanted to be healed because he waited with patience and determination, constantly near the pool despite the fact that others always got in ahead of him. Reading about this story, my mind went immediately to the following passage from Luke 18:2–5 (NLT):

> "There was a judge in a certain city," [Jesus]
> said, "who neither feared God nor cared about

people. A widow of that city came to him repeatedly, saying, 'Give me justice in this dispute with my enemy.' The judge ignored her for a while, but finally he said to himself, 'I don't fear God or care about people, but this woman is driving me crazy. I'm going to see that she gets justice, because she is wearing me out with her constant requests!'"

Because of my own illnesses, I must stay constant in prayer, with a spirit of determination and faith. Otherwise, my situation would produce a spirit of defeat. It is particularly hard when you are surrounded by people who could help you move forward, but they never offer a hand. This man couldn't make it into the water. The people walking by may have counted him out, believing his life was over, so why waste their time? Yet the man showed both persistence and faith that one day he would make it to that water and be healed. And, more importantly, if a godless judge in the above passage in Luke was willing to respond to constant determination, how much more can we expect from a great and loving God?

If we believe God loves us, then we must know He hears our cries for help. Just as importantly, this man had to let go of the tradition of healing at this pool. When Jesus approached him, he let go of the belief that only the first person into the pool was healed. The water in the pool didn't heal these individuals; God did. Now he was blessed to have Jesus Christ face to face, telling him to trust in him.

Afterward Jesus returned to Jerusalem for one of the Jewish holy days. Inside the city, near the Sheep Gate, was the pool of Bethesda, with five covered porches. Crowds of sick people—blind, lame, or paralyzed—lay on the porches. One of the men lying there had been sick for thirty-eight years. When Jesus saw him and knew he had been ill for a long time, he asked him, "Would you like to get well?" "I can't, sir," the sick man said, "for I have no one to put me into the pool when the water bubbles up. Someone else always gets there ahead of me." Jesus told him, "Stand up, pick up your mat, and walk!" Instantly, the man was healed! He rolled up his sleeping mat and began walking! (John 5:1–9 NLT)

I don't know how many other individuals were left there needing a healing, but Jesus chose to heal this man. Believe it or not, the Bible says nothing about him needing rehab to relearn how to walk. His mind and body were instantly healed—a true miracle of God. Can you imagine meeting the healer, face-to-face, who is capable of not only healing but forgiving all our sins? Well, this man did. He met Jesus Christ, who said to him, "Now you are well; so stop sinning, or something even worse may happen to you" (John 5:14 NLT). Jesus backed up his word by healing the man's legs. Jesus's actions prove that his word is true; he has the power to forgive and heal. The true meaning of our words can be realized only through the actions that back them up.

Reading about the paralyzed man's healing, I saw that some people were happy and praised God for sending a healer with such great authority (Matthew 9:8). Yet despite such a miracle, some Jewish leaders objected. John 5:10–11 (NLT) notes this: "'You can't work on the Sabbath! The law doesn't allow you to carry that sleeping mat!' But [the healed man] replied, 'The man who healed me told me, 'Pick up your mat and walk.'"

This story shows me that some individuals in that day could care less whether a person was healed or not. This man had not walked in thirty-eight years, but now he was walking. Suddenly, he could care for himself mentally, physically, and financially, but this meant absolutely nothing to some individuals. The Pharisees in this passage acted as if they cared more about the rules than the life and health of a human being.

People who have never suffered a sick day in their life may find it difficult to visualize struggling with an illness for thirty-eight years. Well, I can. I know that, if we aren't careful, living with illness can become an acceptable way of life. But this is not the life we can have through hope in Jesus Christ. I have not met Jesus face-to-face. However, through the working of the Holy Spirit, I feel as if I have, and meeting him allows me to see God. This has been a blessing in my life.

It may seem as if no one was willing to help the lame or paralyzed man, and it will seem at times that there is no one there for you. In some instances, there may not be anyone humanly present. Therefore, you might lose whatever hope and fight you had at the beginning of your illness. Sadly, this has been my reality at times. But don't let it get to your heart, because it can cause discouragement.

I admit—that's easier to say than to do. Fortunately, Paul shows us how to keep our thoughts on the right path:

> Do not be anxious about anything, but in every situation, by prayer and petition, with thanksgiving, present your requests to God. And the peace of God, which transcends all understanding, will guard your hearts and your minds in Christ Jesus. Finally, brothers and sisters, whatever is true, whatever is

noble, whatever is right, whatever is pure, whatever is lovely, whatever is admirable—if anything is excellent or praiseworthy—think about such things. Whatever you have learned or received or heard from me, or seen in me—put it into practice. And the God of peace will be with you. (Philippians 4:6–9)

Paul instructs us to ask God to help us turn our worries, fears, and doubts into prayers. Above all, read and study the Word of God and pray. I will add this to Paul's advice: putting God's Word into practice is how I came to know the truth in His Word. On the other hand, television, books, movies, and the like can influence my behavior, thoughts, words, and faith in the will of God. He wants me and the world to know that everything I achieve is through Him and no one else.

But what about discouragement? I have found myself in some bad situations of my own making. In fact, I now realize I may have had some control over some of the pain caused by my mental illness. Although we may not have any control over our situation, we do have control over our reactions. These reactions say a lot about our character and our faith in God, which determine our ability to survive or overcome our circumstances.

So far in this book I have not spoken of one person who in my mind did not have reasons to be discouraged. That said, because of the harm it can cause to some individuals, including myself, I want to offer some information on discouragement.

What Is Discouragement?

Let's take a moment to look at a definition of

discouragement. Dictionaries define discouragement as being deprived of courage or self-confidence or saddened by repeated failure.

Our generation did not invent discouragement. Rather, we see it and its consequences as far back as the book of Genesis. But God, who never changes, specializes in doing the impossible in the life of the scum, the outcast, the overlooked, and the ones who are counted out. God can turn a nobody into a somebody.

Discouragement Can Become a Weapon of the Enemy

People such as me, living with mental disorders, are believed by some to be doubly challenged. We struggle with the symptoms of our illnesses, challenged by stereotypes and prejudice. As a result, many of us are overlooked by society and can be robbed of opportunities that define a quality life. Whether or not you admit it or believe it, many people maintain social distance from those of us living with mental disorders. Not because of facts or truths but because of their misconceptions about our disorders.

Christians, like everyone else, will face many trials and tribulations that may be unknown and unseen to the outside world. We fight within as we try to fit into our world. But these fights are not hopeless struggles. They are the precursors of the victory Paul describes in Romans 8:37 (NLT): "No, despite all these things, overwhelming victory is ours through Christ, who loved us." The most effective weapon Satan has used against me is not my limitations but my discouragement regarding my inadequacies. What about you? Discouragement can make you forget who controls your life. It can be a risky road to travel.

Discouragement can also cause you to play the blame

game, pointing at everyone and everything but yourself. As you're unable to move forward, these feelings can turn to bitterness, which grows and takes root in our hearts. During these times, we need to turn to God, confess our struggles, and ask Him for help. Then we must make up our mind to allow the power of the Holy Spirit to lead and guide us through these painful circumstances.

God does not ignore individuals who struggle with communication and who don't know what to ask of God or how. Romans 8:26–30 shows us that God knows our weakness and is ready to help:

> In the same way, the Spirit helps us in our weakness. We do not know what we ought to pray for, but the Spirit himself intercedes for us through wordless groans. And he who searches our hearts knows the mind of the

Spirit, because the Spirit intercedes for God's people in accordance with the will of God. And we know that in all things God works for the good of those who love him, who have been called according to his purpose. For those God foreknew he also predestined to be conformed to the image of his Son, that he might be the firstborn among many brothers and sisters. And those he predestined, he also called; those he called, he also justified; those he justified, he also glorified.

Many of us still struggle and need the assistance of Holy Spirit. When people are discouraged, we often say the wrong things, think the wrong things, and see the wrong things. This can result in counting ourselves out without any help from others.

Saying the Wrong Things

Sometimes, if we are not careful, we can forget who we are and how we got where we are in life. This can lead to discouragement. As a result, we may say and think the wrong things. When and if this happens, we have no one to blame but ourselves. In Numbers 21:4–5, we read what happened to the people of Israel:

> They traveled from Mount Hor along the route to the Red Sea, to go around Edom. But the people grew impatient on the way; they spoke against God and against Moses, and said, "Why have you brought us up out of Egypt to die in the wilderness? There is no bread! There is no water! And we detest this

miserable food!"

Now read God's response to their words:

Then the Lord sent venomous snakes among
them; they bit the people and many Israelites
died. The people came to Moses and said,
"We sinned when we spoke against the Lord
and against you. Pray that the Lord will take
the snakes away from us." So Moses prayed
for the people. The Lord said to Moses, "Make
a snake and put it up on a pole; anyone who is
bitten can look at it and live." So Moses made
a bronze snake and put it up on a pole. Then
when anyone was bitten by a snake and
looked at the bronze snake, they lived.
(Numbers 21:6–9)

Discouragement was the root of Israel's complaining. They seem to have forgotten the situation they were in before God brought them out of slavery. How often do we forget the things God has already done in our lives? How often do we forget what got us into a bad situation?

Studying the book of Numbers carried me to Psalm 78, where we can learn the source of Israel's complaining. They had not been faithful to God. They forgot the miracles God had done for them. God's faithfulness to them was undeniable. Therefore, He used poisonous snakes to punish them for their unbelief and complaining. The lesson in the next passage is so important that Paul used it to warn us about unfaithfulness and failure to put our trust in God:

Nevertheless, God was not pleased with most of them; their bodies were scattered in the wilderness. Now these things occurred as examples to keep us from setting our hearts on evil things as they did. Do not be idolaters, as some of them were; as it is written: "The people sat down to eat and drink and got up to indulge in revelry." We should not commit sexual immorality, as some of them did—and in one day twenty-three thousand of them died. We should not test Christ, as some of them did—and were killed by snakes. And do not grumble, as some of them did—and were killed by the destroying angel. These things happened to them as examples and were written down as warnings for us, on whom the culmination of the ages has come. So, if you think you are standing firm, be careful that you don't fall! (1 Corinthians 10:5–12)

The Bible says nothing about these people being discouraged, but my own experience makes me think they were complaining and discouraged over a situation they themselves had caused. Either way, as we can read, God wasted no time in judging their behavior.

Whenever I let discouragement enter my heart, it produces unbelief, which limits my growth. My obedience to God diminishes my discouragement, and it will do the same for you. This is why I can see what happened to the above individuals. When we are discouraged, we often say words that we will regret later, but spoken words cannot be taken back. If we are saying the wrong things, we are first thinking the wrong things, as Proverbs 23:7 says: "For as he thinketh in his heart, so is he" (KJV). In Luke 6:45, Jesus teaches us that our words and actions reveal our beliefs, attitudes, and motivations:

"A good man out of the good treasure of his
heart bringeth forth that which is good; and an
evil man out of the evil treasure of his heart
bringeth forth that which is evil: for of the
abundance of the heart his mouth
speaketh."(KJV)

See the Wrong Things

Whenever we leave God out of our plans or take our
eyes off Jesus, we have a greater chance of becoming
discouraged. Then our problems appear bigger than they are.
For example, in Numbers 13, beginning with the first verse,
God instructed Moses to send men (scouts) to check out the
Promised Land. God had told the Israelites that the Promised

Land was rich and fertile, and He also promised this land would be theirs.

Following God's instructions, Moses sent out twelve men, one leader from each tribe. When the men returned and reported to Moses, they gave many good reasons for entering the Promised Land. But some couldn't stop talking about the giants they saw, who had frightened them.

They gave Moses this account: "We went into the land to which you sent us, and it does flow with milk and honey! Here is its fruit. But the people who live there are powerful, and the cities are fortified and very large. We even saw descendants of Anak there. The Amalekites live in the Negev; the Hittites, Jebusites and Amorites live in the hill country; and the Canaanites live near the sea and along the Jordan." Then Caleb silenced the people before Moses and said, "We should go up and take possession of the land, for we can certainly do it." But the men who had gone up with him said, "We can't attack those people; they are stronger than we are." And they spread among the Israelites a bad report about the land they had explored. They said, "The land we explored devours those living in it. All the people we saw there are of great size. We saw the Nephilim there (the descendants of Anak come from the Nephilim). We seemed like grasshoppers in our own eyes, and we looked the same to them." (Numbers 13:27–33)

Voicing negative opinions has the potential to impact the people around you. And the negative views of a few can cause you to lose of sight of the positive things God promised. The negative view of just one person can cause confusion and doubt about situations or projects that God has for you. When the Israelites heard this negative report, it made some in the camp forget all the promises God had made to them, especially His promise to help. Read the next passage and see how other individuals were influenced by the discouraging words of ten of the scouts.

"Then the whole community began weeping aloud, and they cried all night. Their voices rose in a great chorus of protest against Moses and Aaron. "If only we had died in Egypt, or even here in the wilderness!" they complained. "Why is the Lord taking us to this country only to have us die in battle? Our wives and our little ones will be carried off as plunder! Wouldn't it be better for us to return to Egypt?" Then they plotted among themselves, "Let's choose a new leader and go back to Egypt!" (Numbers 14:1–4 NLT)

If we allow it, discouragement can blind us to God's power to help and make us doubt the Word of God:

God is not a man, that he should lie; neither the son of man, that he should repent: hath he said, and shall he not do it? or hath he spoken, and shall he not make it good? (Numbers 23:19 KJV)

Caleb and Joshua saw the same sights the others scouts saw, but they said God was greater than all the obstacles they had seen in the land. This revealed their faith in God and His abilities.

> They said to all the people of Israel, "The land we traveled through and explored is a wonderful land! And if the Lord is pleased with us, he will bring us safely into that land and give it to us. It is a rich land flowing with milk and honey. Do not rebel against the Lord, and don't be afraid of the people of the land. They are only helpless prey to us! They have no protection, but the Lord is with us! Don't be afraid of them!" (Numbers 14:7–9 NLT)

The faith Joshua displayed in the above passage did
not change after he entered the Promised Land. He realized
he was serving the same God who had kept every promise He
had made to Moses. God had promise him as He promised
Moses that no one could stand their ground against him as
long as he lived. "For I will be with you as I was with Moses.
I will not fail you or abandon you" (Joshua 1:5 NLT).
Joshua's faith in God led him to ask God for a miracle that
would involve the supernatural power of God. Realizing who
God is and knowing the need for more daylight to win the
battle against their enemies, he asked for something that God
alone could give.

On the day the Lord gave the Israelites victory
over the Amorites, Joshua prayed to the Lord
in front of all the people of Israel. He said,
"Let the sun stand still over Gibeon, and the

moon over the valley of Aijalon." So the sun stood still and the moon stayed in place until the nation of Israel had defeated its enemies. Is this event not recorded in *The Book of Jashar*? The sun stayed in the middle of the sky, and it did not set as on a normal day. There has never been a day like this one before or since, when the Lord answered such a prayer. Surely the Lord fought for Israel that day! (Joshua 10:12–14 NLT)

Israel's enemies may have realized that the Israelites fought better in the daylight. They also knew that nighttime had to come. Since the enemies were better night-fighters, they may have assumed they had won this battle. But Joshua had a plan, and the plan was to put an impossible situation in the hand of God, where all things are possible. Joshua asked for what he needed and wanted, and God gave it!

This is the mind-set God wants from us when we look at our circumstances. No matter how big or bad our obstacles may appear, we must believe God is greater. "Ye are of God, little children, and have overcome them: because greater is He that is in you, than he that is in the world" (1 John 4:4 KJV). Thus, you and I should have the same faith as Caleb and Joshua. Unlike these two men, we have the Bible, and we know Jesus Christ is the only-begotten Son of God.

Discouragement can also influence us to push others away, even loved ones who are trying to assist us in our struggles. This can greatly influence our outlook on life. For me, it can feel like a dark cloud hanging over me, with no sign of light anywhere. Discouragement can steal our joy, motivation, and any hope we have to use our God-given talents. But in the midst of discouragement, hope can come to us through Jesus Christ.

> Why am I discouraged? Why is my heart so sad? I will put my hope in God! I will praise him again—my Savior and my God! Now I am deeply discouraged, but I will remember you—even from distant Mount Hermon, the source of the Jordan, from the land of Mount Mizar. I hear the tumult of the raging seas as your waves and surging tides sweep over me. But each day the Lord pours his unfailing love upon me, and through each night I sing his songs, praying to God who gives me life.
> (Psalm 43:5–8 NLT)

Self-worth comes when we realize who we are in Jesus Christ. Reaching this point allows for total surrender to his power and gives us hope for the future. Total surrender is not a bad thing, as I hope you see in the lives of the individuals mentioned in this chapter.

Chapter Four: Counted Out by Those in Power

We have no control over some things in our lives. In my first book, I spoke on this topic in regard to our families. My next subjects are Ishmael and his mother Hagar, and they may be perfect examples. Their lives were controlled by those in power. Ishmael started out with some power and importance because of his birthright, but that changed quickly.

Ishmael's story teaches us how quickly everything can change in our lives. These changes can come through illness, divorce, loss of loved ones, loss of a job, or any unanticipated situation. They can alter our whole life. The story of Ishmael shows us how decisions made without God's guidance can have lasting effects from generation to generation.

Let's look back at those who are in power in this story: Abram (the father of faith) and his wife Sarai. (Abram's name was later changed to Abraham by God, and Sarai's name changed to Sarah, in Genesis 18:15.)

Abraham was a chosen servant of God who had servants of his own. Abraham's servants' condition was similar to or even worse than that of slaves. They were his property to be bought and sold or given as any other property he owned. In Chapter 17 of Genesis, God gives Abraham direct instructions concerning not only his family but also his servants:

> He who is eight days old among you shall be circumcised, every male child in your generations, he who is born in your house or bought with money from any foreigner who is not your descendant. He who is born in your

house and he who is bought with your money

must be circumcised, and My covenant shall

be in your flesh for an everlasting covenant.

And the uncircumcised male child, who is not

circumcised in the flesh of his foreskin, that

person shall be cut off from his people; he has

broken My covenant." (Genesis 17:12–14

NKJV)

In order to have a better understanding of this story,

we must look at Sarai, who was barren. Because of Sarai's

age, she was no longer expected to have children. She

proposed that Abram take another wife, for the children of

such a union, through a slave woman, would be Sarai's

property. She did this without asking counsel from God,

which shows her disbelief of God's promise to give them a

child. The problem, it seemed, was that God did not provide

them a date or time. Since He knows our beginning and ending and is the creator of time, He knows just how much time you and I have. But I read nothing about Abram refusing this offer. Let's read what the Bible says about his response:

> Abram agreed to what Sarai said. So after Abram had been living in Canaan ten years, Sarai his wife took her Egyptian slave Hagar and gave her to her husband to be his wife. He slept with Hagar, and she conceived. (Genesis 16:2–4)

Taking matters into our hands can cause great pain and lasting consequences, as we read in this story. In fact, our lack of faith in God to fulfill His promise can take us in the wrong direction. I spoke about this happening to me in my first book. I took a matter into my own hands. As a result, I lost time and money I did not have to spare. Exactly like Sarai, I went about trying to do it my way. My disobedience prevented me from spending time with my family. In this story, Sarai and Abram's disobedience resulted in pain for those they loved.

Sarai soon became angry with Abram, but she was the one who started this thing. Soon she started playing the blame game, with two other lives involved through no fault of their own.

> When she knew she was pregnant, she began
> to despise her mistress. Then Sarai said to
> Abram, "You are responsible for the wrong I
> am suffering. I put my slave in your arms, and
> now that she knows she is pregnant, she
> despises me. May the Lord judge between you

and me." "Your slave is in your hands,"

Abram said. "Do with her whatever you think

best." Then Sarai mistreated Hagar; so she

fled from her. (Genesis 16:4–6)

In Sarai's defense, I have found that it is easier to

blame others than to look at our own mistakes and ask God

for the forgiveness that allows us to move forward. Still, she

could do only so much to Abram. Then again, she could take

out her frustration on her servant Hagar with his permission.

When Sarai complained to Abram about the conduct of her

servant, he gave her authority to do as she pleased with her.

Hagar had no control over the plans set in motion by

those in authority over her. She did, however, have control

over her own behavior, which at first appeared to have gotten

her into trouble. But let's be real. Sarai was not happy about

the fact that another woman was carrying her husband's

baby, even if it was her idea. This is something I hear about a lot in our society. For many women who are unable to conceive or carry a pregnancy to term, surrogacy is a viable option. Considering the agreement between Sarai and Abram, I would say surrogacy existed before our time.

Yet, this was not the issue with Sarai. At this point, we do not know whether she could carry a baby full term or not. The Bible says does say in Genesis 11:30 that she was barren. Still, knowing that she was not getting any younger may have motivated her to take on of the role of God. We often are quick to look at our age or the age of others and decide that certain tasks are too much for our advancing age. This is why the working of God's supernatural power is still, to this day, a central part of my survival. The story of Abram and Sarai completely changed my views about age.

No one can doubt that this had to have been a stressful situation, even if it was unavoidable. Hagar chose to

behave in a manner unpleasing to her boss. Maybe carrying
the baby of old Abram went to her head and made her think
she was now as good as Sarai. Or better, since now she had a
child and Sarai couldn't conceive. I don't know what she was
thinking, but at one time in my life I did think I was better
than others. This was when I really was crazy but didn't
know it. I know I am acting with better sense now because of
the Holy Spirit.

Perhaps Hagar soon learned that carrying old
Abram's baby gave her no more power than she had before.
She was still a servant under authority. In her distress, Hagar
ran from her mistress and her problem.

But we all must confront our problems, because
running away never solves any problem and may open the
door to others. In the passage below, we read that God sent
an angel to speak to Hagar. The angel didn't approve of

Hagar's behavior but told her to go back. He also informed her about the child she was carrying:

> The angel of the Lord found Hagar near a spring in the desert; it was the spring that is beside the road to Shur. And he said, "Hagar, servant of Sarai, where have you come from, and where are you going?" "I'm running away from my mistress Sarai," she answered. Then the angel of the Lord told her, "Go back to your mistress and submit to her." The angel added, "I will so increase your descendants that they will be too numerous to count." The angel also said to her, "You are now with child and you will have a son. You shall name him Ishmael, for the Lord has heard of your misery." (Genesis 16:7–11)

From reading this story, we can conclude that three people made serious mistakes. Abram went along with Sarai's plan, and she took the matter into her hands. The situation got even worse when he refused to act or help solve the problem for which he was somewhat to blame. And Hagar did not control her attitude.

Despite all their issues, Hagar, Sarai, and Abram got a son. Even in the midst of our own messes and the mistakes made for us by others, God can solve our problem. Abram did not have the courage to solve this problem he helped create. God, however, had no difficulty helping these troubled people. No mess is too big for Him to repair if we let Him help us.

As said previously, Hagar was a servant, but no less important to God. Hagar obeyed and did what the angel of God told her to do. Yet I find nowhere in the Bible that

Abram or anyone else went looking for her when she ran away. Thank God He knew where she was. He made sure she was taken care of. This would not be the last time God would care for her.

According to the Bible, Abraham was eighty-six years old when Ishmael was born via Sarai's plan. But thirteen years later, Sarai gave birth, through a miracle of God, to Isaac.

Suddenly Ishmael was no longer the only son. During the time Sarah had been barren, Hagar bragged about her child. When Isaac was weaned, Ishmael mocked his half brother. Angered, Sarah told Abraham to cast the two out.

> But Sarah saw that the son whom Hagar the
> Egyptian had borne to Abraham was mocking,
> and she said to Abraham, "Get rid of that
> slave woman and her son, for that woman's

son will never share in the inheritance with

my son Isaac." The matter distressed Abraham

greatly because it concerned his son. But God

said to him, "Do not be so distressed about the

boy and your slave woman. Listen to whatever

Sarah tells you, because it is through Isaac

that your offspring will be reckoned."

(Genesis 21:9–12)

The Bible says that Abraham obeyed God. He got up

the next morning and sent Hagar and Ishmael from his home

into the wilderness with food and a container of water. One

container of water for two people. You would think that, with

all Abraham's wealth, he would have given the woman more

than just enough water for one day. Maybe this was all God

told him to give her because God Himself had others plans

for this little family. They may have been counted out by the ones in power in Abraham's house, but the One who has power over the house and the man of the house was about to take care of her and her son without anyone's assistance.

As Hagar wandered in Beersheba without direction and without water for her and the child, she was now again in distress, abandoned by those who should have cared for her. God, however, did not abandon Hagar and her child. They were indeed stranded in the desert of Beersheba, dying from thirst, but they would not die. God had not said it was over.

When the water was gone, she put the boy in the shade of a bush. Then she went and sat down by herself about a hundred yards away. "I don't want to watch the boy die," she said, as she burst into tears. But God heard the boy crying, and the angel of God called to Hagar from heaven, "Hagar, what's wrong? Do not be afraid! God has heard the boy crying as he lies there. Go to him and comfort him, for I will make a great nation from his descendants." Then God opened Hagar's eyes, and she saw a well full of water. She quickly filled her water container and gave the boy a drink. And God was with the boy as he grew up in the wilderness. (Genesis 21:15–20 NLT)

Would you like to know what happened to Ishmael? Well, let me tell you. God told Hagar this about her son: "This son of yours will be a wild man, as untamed as a wild donkey! He will raise his fist against everyone, and everyone will be against him. Yes, he will live in open hostility against all his relatives" (Genesis 16:12 NLT).

Ishmael became a skillful archer, settling in the wilderness of Paran, and a ruler of a large tribe. Hagar arranged for Ishmael to marry an Egyptian woman. Scholars also suggest that the Ishmaelites were nomads living in the wilderness of Sinai and Paran, south of Israel. One of Ishmael's daughters married Esau.

> And Esau seeing that the daughters of Canaan
>
> pleased not Isaac his father;
>
> then went Esau unto Ishmael, and took unto
>
> the wives which he had Mahalath the daughter
>
> of Ishmael Abraham's son, the sister of
>
> Nebajoth, to be his wife. (Genesis 28:8–9
>
> KJV)

According to Psalm 83:4–7 (KJV), the Ishmaelites were hostile to Israel and to God:

They have said, Come, and let us cut them off
from being a nation; that the name of Israel
may be no more in remembrance. For they
have consulted together with one consent:
they are confederate against thee: the
tabernacles of Edom, and the Ishmaelites; of
Moab, and the Hagarenes; Gebal, and
Ammon, and Amalek; the Philistines with the
inhabitants of Tyre.

We can also read about Ishmael again after the death
of his father, Abraham. The Bible says he joined with Isaac
to bury their father in a cave of Machpelah near Mamre, in
the field of Ephron son of Zohar the Hittite, where Sarah was
also buried (Genesis 25:9). In the beginning of Genesis
chapter 25 you can read that Abraham left everything he had
to Isaac, but before his death, he gave gifts to the sons of his

concubines and sent them off to the east, away from Isaac. I find nothing that says Abraham left anything to Ishmael, unless Hagar was considered a concubine and not an Egyptian servant in these passages. Nonetheless, Ishmael fathered twelve sons, who became the rulers of twelve tribes (Genesis 25:16).

Ishmael lived to be 137 years old, despite the obstacles surrounding his birth, his youth, others' opinions of him and his situation, and the lack of a birthright. God took care of him, and He will do the same for you and me. Those who saw the Egyptian servant being led away from Abraham's house that day may have believed it was all over for Hagar and her child. Who would take in a servant with a child? Their survival may have appeared impossible to the human eye. I am thankful that in her situation, as well as mine and maybe yours, the Word of God says otherwise. In Deuteronomy 30:8 (NLT), God says to us, "So be strong and courageous! Do not be afraid and do not panic before them. For the Lord your God will personally go ahead of you. He will neither fail you nor abandon you."

We all need to thank God that He has the last word over our lives.

Chapter Five: Counted Out by Brothers and Those in Authority

Now let's look at another person, one who was counted out by his own brothers. If you are dealing with an issue like this, don't feel you are the first or will be the last. Just be thankful that God has the last say-so about your life, and don't give up.

Several messages in Joseph's life speak to me as a parent or grandparent, because the root of his brothers' actions in this story is jealousy, envy, and hatred.

Joseph was the son of Jacob and Rachel. These two had a remarkable love story. Perhaps this was why Jacob loved him as he did, not to mention that Jacob was old when Joseph was born. Let's stop for a moment and look at the history of Joseph's parents.

Jacob's father, Isaac, sent him from his homeland to the land of his uncle. There he was to marry one of his uncle's daughters because his father did not want him to marry a Canaanite woman. But Jacob was also on the run because, with the help of his mother, he had tricked his twin brother out of his birthright by lying to their father. (These were the first twins cited in the Bible.) In that day, the birthright was a special honor given to the firstborn and included a double portion of the family's inheritance. If the oldest son sold or gave away this birthright, he would lose not only his position of leadership but also material goods.

One day when Jacob was cooking some stew, Esau arrived home from the wilderness exhausted and hungry. Esau said to Jacob, "I'm starved! Give me some of that red stew!" (This is how Esau got his other name, Edom, which means "red.") "All right," Jacob replied, "but trade me your rights as the firstborn son." "Look, I'm dying of starvation!" said Esau. "What good is my birthright to me now?" But Jacob said, "First you must swear that your birthright is mine." So Esau swore an oath, thereby selling all his rights as the firstborn to his brother, Jacob. (Genesis 25:29–33 NLT)

Acting on impulse, Esau sold his birthright for food. This reminds me of grocery shopping when I'm hungry. I buy everything I want, selecting items from almost every aisle as if I planned to feed fifty people or more. But much later, I realize it wasn't what I wanted, needed, or could afford. In Esau's case, his brother Jacob was there, willing and ready to take advantage of Esau's weakness.

Later, Esau hated his brother Jacob because, as noted in Genesis 27:41, Jacob had stolen his blessing. He decided to kill Jacob as soon as their father was dead and gone.

Rereading this next passage, I realized that Esau and Jacob's

mother were behind all these schemes and lies.

> When Rebekah was told what her older son
>
> Esau had said, she sent for her younger son
>
> Jacob and said to him, "Your brother Esau is
>
> consoling himself with the thought of killing
>
> you. Now then, my son, do what I say: Flee at
>
> once to my brother Laban in Haran. Stay with
>
> him for a while until your brother's fury
>
> subsides. When your brother is no longer
>
> angry with you and forgets what you did to
>
> him, I'll send word for you to come back from
>
> there. Why should I lose both of you in one
>
> day?" Then Rebekah said to Isaac, "I'm
>
> disgusted with living because of these Hittite

women. If Jacob takes a wife from among the

women of this land, from Hittite women like

these, my life will not be worth living."

(Genesis 27:42–46)

Studying the situation with this family, I made

another important observation. Esau and his mother each

failed to accept their role in this whole affair. Esau refused to

acknowledge the cause of the trouble: his willingness to give

away his birthright for food. Rachel wouldn't admit to

plotting behind her husband's back to get the birthright for

her younger son, Jacob. We see here how blame-shifting

blinded this family from seeing the real issues. I spoke earlier

about blaming other people for our mistakes and the danger it

can cause.

Jacob, with the help of his mother, received the

blessings he wanted by fooling his brother and lying to his

father. However, things did not go as he had planned. In addition, Jacob's mother was willing to deceive her husband and hurt Esau in order to get what she wanted for her favorite son, Jacob. Satan never tells us the result of our sins!

Usually, when we mess up, we think nothing about the results until they hit us in the face. I don't want to spend too much time talking about Jacob, but I do want you to have some understanding of what went on before Jacob met the woman who would become the mother of Joseph. Jacob's favoritism of Rachel over Leah may have been the root of his favoring her sons.

Upon arriving in the land where his uncle lived, Jacob encountered Rachel before he met his uncle or the older sister. Genesis 29:11 (NLT) says, "Then Jacob kissed Rachel, and he wept aloud." A first kiss, and the man cries. Not Rachel, but Jacob.

But we must consider two important customs of that day. First, a man desiring a wife had to present a dowry. Jacob didn't have one, but he could work. He agreed to work seven years for Rachel. Second, the older sister had to be married first. But like Jacob, his uncle Laban was deceitful, and withheld this information from Jacob. Laban fooled Jacob into working the first seven years and thinking he was working for Rachel. But instead he got the older sister, Leah. Jacob agreed to work another seven years for Rachel. He worked fourteen years for this woman, so it was clear that he loved Rachel.

If you read Genesis 27, you'll recall how Jacob fooled his own father and what the results of his actions were. Still, remember not to be quick to judge. Although Jacob was a liar and trickster, God was not done with him yet. During the last days of his life, Jacob became a grabber. The Bible says he grabbed on to God and would not let go (Genesis 32:22–32)

God became important to him, and he finally realized his need for God in his life. During this stage, God changed Jacob's name to Israel. He was blessed by God and was a blessing to God. Can you and I say the same?

> And God said to him, "I am God Almighty; be
> fruitful and increase in number. A nation and
> a community of nations will come from you,
> and kings will be among your descendants.
> The land I gave to Abraham and Isaac I also
> give to you, and I will give this land to your
> descendants after you." (Genesis 35:11–12)

From the life of Jacob I learned the root of my strongest convictions. You may read it many times in my writing because it drives me to act, to move, and to hope. No manner how I started out in life and no matter how many trials and difficulties I've experienced while living with mental disorders, the new life I now live is a tribute to God. I have a burning need and desire to stay as close to God as I can, despite all I go through and have to deal with. I only hope you can say the same.

Joseph

Let's look closely at Joseph who, around the age of seventeen, was working with his half brothers, tending their father's flocks. He was what we old people used to call a tattletale. He made sure his father knew all the bad things his brothers did (Genesis 37:2). Anyone with siblings knows his brothers didn't receive this well. The brothers already hated Joseph, so telling their father about the bad things they did behind his back made things even worse.

In my opinion as a parent and a grandparent, Jacob did nothing to help the situation. You would think he would have done all in his power to avoid divisiveness between his children. But no, Jacob's past experience of favoritism passed on to the next generation. Jacob's mother favored him and his father favored the older brother, Esau (Genesis 25:27–28 NLT). Honestly, I don't think any of this came to

Jacob's mind. If it had, I would think he would have handled the situation differently. And he certainly wouldn't have given Joseph an expensive robe, ensuring that the favoritism would continue.

Biblical scholars suggest that this was not a simple robe. This particular robe was the kind worn by royalty—ankle length, with long sleeves and lots of color. To Jacob's other sons, the robe was an emblem of his love for Joseph. Giving this kind of robe to Joseph heightened the strained relationships between his sons and himself.

As a parent, I know that I have no control over my feelings about my children or grandchildren. But I can control my actions and how I treat my family. Because of Jacob's actions and his favoritism toward Joseph, the older brothers resented him to the point of hatred (Genesis 37:3–4 NLT).

Joseph made matters worse when he began relating his dreams. These foretelling visions showed him ruling over his family one day.

One night Joseph had a dream, and when he told his brothers about it, they hated him more than ever. "Listen to this dream," he said. "We were out in the field, tying up bundles of grain. Suddenly my bundle stood up, and your bundles all gathered around and bowed low before mine!" His brothers responded, "So you think you will be our king, do you? Do you actually think you will reign over us?" And they hated him all the more because of his dreams and the way he talked about them. Soon Joseph had another dream, and again he told his brothers about it. "Listen, I have had another dream," he said. "The sun, moon, and eleven stars bowed low before me!" This time he told the dream to his father as well as to his brothers, but his father scolded him. "What kind of dream is that?" he asked. "Will your mother and I and your brothers actually come and bow to the ground before you?" (Genesis 37:5-10 NLT)

The bitterness toward Joseph peaked as he himself fueled the fire with what his brothers believed was boasting. Can you imagine the young boy having authority over his oldest brothers? Even in my day, my mother gave me full authority over all my siblings. And in the Old Testament, the firstborn son normally received a double inheritance and took over his father's role as head of the family. But sometimes God reverses this tradition, as He did with Jacob and Esau.

And much later, when Jacob blessed Joseph's boys, Manasseh and Ephraim, he gave the greater birthrights to the younger son (Genesis 48:8–20).

When God gets ready to choose people for His plans, He looks past the traditions, appearances, and positions that leave most of us in awe. To be completely honest, I am still flabbergasted that God called me to be an author!

Joseph was a young man at this time, spoiled by his father, and had not learned that we cannot repeat everything that God tells us. When God reveals His plans for us, we have to understand that not everyone is going to be happy for us. Also, Joseph had not yet learned that everything we have comes from God, including our talent. But just like me, he would later learn through hardship and give God the credit He deserves.

Joseph's hardship started when his brothers, who labeled him the "dreamer," plotted to kill him in the wilderness. But Reuben, the oldest brother, objected to outright murder.

> When Reuben heard this, he tried to rescue him from their hands. "Let's not take his life," he said. "Don't shed any blood. Throw him into this cistern here in the desert, but don't lay a hand on him." Reuben said this to rescue him from them and take him back to his father. (Genesis 37:21–22)

Sometime later during this discussion, the brothers agreed to sell Joseph as a slave and mislead their father into thinking his favorite son had been slain by wild animals.

> As they sat down to eat their meal, they looked up and saw a caravan of Ishmaelites

coming from Gilead. Their camels were loaded with spices, balm and myrrh, and they were on their way to take them down to Egypt. Judah said to his brothers, "What will we gain if we kill our brother and cover up his blood? Come, let's sell him to the Ishmaelites and not lay our hands on him; after all, he is our brother, our own flesh and blood." His brothers agreed. So when the Midianite merchants came by, his brothers pulled Joseph up out of the cistern and sold him for twenty shekels of silver to the Ishmaelites, who took him to Egypt. (Genesis 37:25–28)

According to the Bible, Reuben was not present when the other brothers sold Joseph into slavery. But when he found out, he went along with the plans they'd put in place to fool their father. When Reuben returned and saw that Joseph was not in the pit, it appears to me that his first thoughts were not about Joseph's well-being but rather worry for himself: "Then he went back to his brothers and lamented, "The boy is gone! What will I do now?" (Genesis 37:30 NLT).

While selling Joseph into slavery may have sounded better than killing him, I don't believe these brothers expected Joseph to survive. They were willing and ready to kill their own brother over a robe and some dreams. According to biblical scholars, his brothers may not have killed him, but they were willing to let cruel slave traders do their dirty work for them. To cover up their evil actions, they all agreed to deceive their father into believing his favorite son was dead.

Writing this brings my mind back to the time Jacob deceived his own father. Although Joseph's life changed and he was blessed through his connection with God, he suffered the consequences of his sins. Just as with Jacob, God may not punish us immediately for our sins, but the punishments will surely come if we don't repent. Because we have mercy and Jesus Christ, though, He doesn't punish us according to what we deserve.

What Joseph's brothers didn't know is the same thing people today fail to realize: God has plans in place for our lives, and no man can alter them. God had the last word regarding Joseph's life and those of his brothers. But in the meantime, God's plans for Joseph began with difficult, frightening, and uncertain days. And yet, Joseph shows us that our faith in God can protect and sustain us.

When Joseph arrived in Egypt, Potiphar bought him. Potiphar was a member of Pharaoh's personal staff. Joseph was blessed by God, who allowed him to find favor with Potiphar. Potiphar liked Joseph so much that he appointed him the supervisor of Potiphar's household, entrusting him with the handling of his business. According to the Bible, "from the day Joseph was put in charge of his master's household and property, the Lord began to bless Potiphar's household for Joseph's sake" (Genesis 39:5 NLT). Is this great or what? You and I can be blessed because of the way we treat those God places in our paths.

Joseph had a problem though—Potiphar's wife, who also liked Joseph. In fact, she liked him just as much as her husband, but in a different way. Therefore, Potiphar's wife invited Joseph to sleep with her. I know a lot of men who would have taken her up on this offer. However, we can see the uniqueness of this young man who refused her advances.

> "With me in charge," he told her, "my master does not concern himself with anything in the house; everything he owns he has entrusted to my care. No one is greater in this house than I

am. My master has withheld nothing from me
except you, because you are his wife. How
then could I do such a wicked thing and sin
against God?" (Genesis 39:8–9)

Notice that Joseph said the sin would be against God.
He did not say it would be against her and Potiphar. God
commands complete abstinence before marriage. Sex
between a husband and his wife is the only form of sexual
relations God approves (Hebrews 13:4).

It appears to me that Joseph did all he could to stay
away from Potiphar's wife. But I can see how this could have
been a difficult task, since she was out to have him in her
bed.

One day he went into the house to attend to
his duties, and none of the household servants

was inside. She caught him by his cloak and said, "Come to bed with me!" But he left his cloak in her hand and ran out of the house. When she saw that he had left his cloak in her hand and had run out of the house, she called her household servants. "Look," she said to them, "this Hebrew has been brought to us to make sport of us! He came in here to sleep with me, but I screamed. When he heard me scream for help, he left his cloak beside me and ran out of the house." She kept his cloak beside her until his master came home. Then she told him this story: "That Hebrew slave you brought us came to me to make sport of me. But as soon as I screamed for help, he left his cloak beside me and ran out of the house." When his master heard the story

his wife told him, saying, "This is how your
slave treated me," he burned with anger.
Joseph's master took him and put him in
prison, the place where the king's prisoners
were confined. (Genesis 39:11–20)

I often see people in the media being led out of prison
for crimes they did not commit. Some of them act as if it's
the worst thing that has ever happened. If that happened to
me or you, we might feel the same was. Joseph had been
betrayed first by his brothers and later by the wife of
Potiphar. And, although he was innocent of the crime
brought against him, he was cast into prison (Genesis 39:20).
Jesus Christ was falsely accused too—he was guilty of no
crime and no sin.

While Joseph was in prison, God touched the heart of
his jailer. Before long, Joseph was in charge of all the other

prisoners and became the prison administrator. I am sure Potiphar's wife, like Joseph's brothers, thought they had seen the last of Joseph. However, God had other plans for this young man. We can begin to see the unfolding of the dreams Joseph told his brothers and father about years ago. In prison, Joseph was blessed by God, not only to have favor with the jailer but also to interpret dreams. First we read about Joseph interpreting the dreams of two other prisoners, a cupbearer and the chief baker. Both interpretations prove to be true, and the cupbearer was later released from jail and restored to his position (40:1–23).

If you read Genesis 40, you will see as I did that in each episode, Joseph kept his focus on God. He did not use any opportunity to try to make himself look good.

The king's dream got Joseph released from prison. Two years after Joseph had interpreted the prisoners' dreams, the king himself had some troubling dreams. Word spread that the king was looking for someone to interpret his dream, and the cupbearer remembered Joseph's gift of interpretation. Had the cupbearer forgotten until that moment that Joseph had the ability to interpret dreams? I don't know. Sometimes it may appear that we are overlooked, but it just may not be God's time for us. And so, at God's time, the cupbearer told the king about Joseph's ability.

In the morning [Pharaoh's] mind was troubled, so he sent for all the magicians and wise men of Egypt. Pharaoh told them his dreams, but no one could interpret them for him. Then the chief cupbearer said to Pharaoh, "Today I am reminded of my shortcomings. Pharaoh was once angry with his servants, and he imprisoned me and the chief baker in the house of the captain of the guard. Each of us had a dream the same night, and each dream had a meaning of its own. Now a young Hebrew was there with us, a servant of the captain of the guard. We told him our dreams, and he interpreted them for us, giving each man the interpretation of his dream. And things turned out exactly as he interpreted them to us: I was restored to my position, and the other man was hanged." So Pharaoh sent for Joseph, and he was quickly brought from the dungeon. When he had shaved and changed his clothes, he came before Pharaoh. (Genesis 41:8–14)

Upon interpreting the Pharaoh's dreams, Joseph predicted seven years of bountiful harvests followed by seven years of severe famine in Egypt. He advised the king to begin storing grain in preparation for the coming dearth. Pharaoh, realizing that Joseph was a man filled with the Spirit of God, made him ruler over Egypt, second only to himself. Pharaoh told Joseph that he was the wisest man in the land. He trusted Joseph enough to say, "I am king, but no one will move a hand or a foot in the entire land of Egypt without the approval of Joseph" (Genesis 41:44 NLT).

It had been a long journey for Joseph, but he never gave up on himself or God. He was seventeen years old when his brothers sold him into slavery. He was in charge of the entire land of Egypt at the age of thirty. Who saw that coming? Not his brothers or the woman who accused him of trying to rape her.

But this was not the end of Joseph's story. His foretelling dreams had not been completely revealed, but they were about to be. When the famine struck, Canaan was affected. Jacob sent ten of his sons to Egypt to buy grain.

When Jacob learned that there was grain in Egypt, he said to his sons, "Why do you just keep looking at each other?" He continued, "I have heard that there is grain in Egypt. Go down there and buy some for us, so that we may live and not die." Then ten of Joseph's brothers went down to buy grain from Egypt. But Jacob did not send Benjamin, Joseph's brother, with the others, because he was afraid that harm might come to him. (Genesis 42:1–4)

While there, they met their long-lost brother, whom they did not recognize. But Joseph recognized them. Joseph's brothers bowed down to him, fulfilling the earlier prophecy.

As a boy, Joseph had boasted about his dreams. As a man he saw no need to, so he kept quiet.

Joseph saw that his only full brother had not suffered the same fate as he had from his brothers. After learning that his father was still alive, he revealed his identity to his brothers and forgave their wrongdoing. Joseph wanted to know whether his brothers had changed their ways before he proved to them that he, like them, was not the same.

Many times in our lives we must deal with distressing circumstances. Some of these may be of our making, or they may be unjust, as they were in Joseph's life. Either way, as we learn from the story of Joseph, we must remain faithful and accept that God is ultimately in control. That way, we can be confident that God will reward our faithfulness in the end. No one would have blamed Joseph if he had turned his brothers away when they were in need. All the same, God desires that we exercise mercy above all other sacrifices we may offer Him (Hosea 6:6; Matthew 9:13).

Joseph's story shows us how God sovereignly works to overcome evil and bring about His plan. After all his ordeals, Joseph was able to see God's hand at work. Can you? As he revealed his identity to his brothers, Joseph spoke of their sin in this manner:

> And now, do not be distressed and do not be angry with yourselves for selling me here, because it was to save lives that God sent me ahead of you. For two years now there has been famine in the land, and for the next five years there will not be plowing and reaping. But God sent me ahead of you to preserve for you a remnant on earth and to save your lives by a great deliverance. So

then, it was not you who sent me here, but God. He made me father to Pharaoh, lord of his entire household and ruler of all Egypt. (Genesis 45:5–8)

Much later, after the death of their father, Joseph again reassured his brothers, offering forgiveness and saying, "As far I am concerned, God turned into good what you meant for evil" (Genesis 50:20). Neither man's nor Satan's most wicked intentions can ever spoil the perfect plan of God. God brought good out of hopeless situations, like the evilness of his brothers and Potiphar's wife. Joseph was forgotten by those he had helped. In what must have been his most difficult and hopeless situations, Joseph held on to his faith in God. God came through for Joseph just as He did for Daniel. Through his pain, suffering, and betrayal, Joseph prepared for the great responsibility God had planned for him.

Joseph's story proves that God can overrule any idea or plan of man or woman if we put our trust in Him. The story of Joseph also validates to me how important we are to God. We should all be thankful that He has the last word regarding not only our lives but also our situations.

Chapter Six: Counted Out by Wife and Friends

The life of Job is a good example of the hope God offers us when our pain and suffering are too deep for us to understand. Job was a godly man. He was a prosperous and blessed farmer with thousands of sheep, camels, and other livestock. Job had a large family and many servants. One day, after Satan had roamed across the earth, God asked him if he had noticed His servant Job. God told Satan that Job was a man of complete integrity who feared Him and would do no evil. Satan then attacked Job's motives for serving God, accusing him of being faithful to Him only because God gave him everything he wanted.

Satan wanted to prove that Job loved God because God had given him a great life. According to Satan, Job was no different from anyone else. Hard times would destroy his superficial faith and reveal his true character. But for Job, as is true of most true believers, hard times brought him closer to God as he took shelter in Him in order to withstand the storms.

This conversation resulted in Job's testing. God allowed Satan to kill Job's children, servants, and livestock and to destroy his home and everything he had. But He would not give Satan permission to harm Job physically. One thing I learned from this dialogue between God and Satan is that God is fully aware of all Satan's attempts to destroy our lives and cause us pain. All believers should know this important fact and hold it dear to our hearts!

In the first of these tests, Satan took all Job's possessions and family. Still, Satan lost this round because Job, who was overwhelmed with loss and grief, acknowledged that everything he had was a gift from God and thus was owned by God. Job's response indicated that he loved God because of who He was, not because he could get things from Him.

> At this, Job got up and tore his robe and shaved his head. Then he fell to the ground in worship and said: "Naked I came from my mother's womb, and naked I will depart. The Lord gave and the Lord has taken away; may the name of the Lord be praised." (Job 1:20–21)

Satan still did not believe Job's motives. So in chapter 2, he went back to God to ask permission to take away Job's health. "A man will give up everything he has to save his life. But reach out and take away his health, and he will surely curse you to your face!" (Job 1:4–5).

Again we see that Satan had to get permission from God to take away Job's health. God gave Satan permission to impose pain but not to take Job's life.

Reading through this story, I noticed something I had not before. Job's wife was spared while the rest of his family was killed. She also suffered because of her loss, and now she was dealing with a sick husband. Therefore, she did not response in the same manner as Job about their situation or about God. Job's wife said to him, "Are you still trying to maintain your integrity? Curse God and die" (Job 2:9 NLT).

Job's wife's words must have caused him even more pain, although her words may have come as the result of her own suffering. Job responded to her in this manner: "You talk like a foolish woman. Should we accept only good things from the hand of God and never anything bad?" (Job 2:10 NLT) I did not read anything about Job's wife's faith in God—only his. So I believe she had given up on Job and her faith in God, if she had any. She may have thought that believing in God protects us from trials and tribulations. Job's story teaches us that it does not, but that we should never give up on God, no matter what. So even despite their pain and loss, Job said nothing bad against his God.

The book of Job helps me understand that Satan has no power over my life. That includes finances, health, death, and physical destruction, unless it is by God's permission. God has power over what Satan can and cannot do. This is beyond my human ability to understand, but suffering is sometimes a means to purify, test, teach, and strengthen the soul. I can honestly say that my illnesses have caused purification of my heart, tested me and my faith, taught me who I could trust and depend on, and strengthened my faith in God.

God deserves and requests our love and praise in all circumstances of life. In the last section, I spoke about discouragement and its danger to our lives. If anyone fits the model for discouragement, it would be Job.

In the beginning of Job's suffering, he said nothing. When his three friends came and sat quietly with him for seven days and seven nights, they too said nothing at first. Sometimes when we don't know what to say or how to speak with compassion, we need to do as Job's friends did at first and say nothing. (Job 2:11–13). By chapter 3, Job decided to speak in response to Satan's second test, but Job did not say anything against God. He did, however, curse the day he was born.

"Why wasn't I born dead? Why didn't I die as I came from the womb? Why was I laid on my mother's lap? Why did she nurse me at her breasts? Had I died at birth, I would now be at peace. I would be asleep and at rest. I would rest with the world's kings and prime ministers, whose great buildings now lie in ruins. I would rest with princes, rich in gold, whose palaces were filled with silver. Why wasn't I buried like a stillborn child, like a baby who never lives to see the light? For in death the wicked cause no trouble, and the weary are at rest. (Job 3:11–17 NLT)

Being forsaken by God was the worst thing that could have happened to Job. During times such as this, we have to dig deep within ourselves to gain the strength God gives us to hold on to our faith. We need to be careful not to misjudge our vulnerability during times of pain and suffering. We must allow the Holy Spirit to keep our eyes on Jesus Christ so we can see hope and relief or hear encouraging words from family or friends, or from within.

At first, Job's friends were quiet, then they tried to console him. Finally, they began to blame him.

Unfortunately, Job's friends did what many of us have done: they jumped to their own conclusions about the root of Job's problem. As with us in many instances, they were wrong. No matter—the first of the three acknowledged that Job had been a source of strength to others. But in the same statement, he blamed Job.

"But now trouble comes to you, and you are discouraged; it strikes you, and you are dismayed. Should not your piety be your confidence and your blameless ways your hope? Consider now: Who, being innocent, has ever perished? Where were the upright ever destroyed? As I have observed, those who plow evil and those who sow trouble reap it. At the breath of God they perish." (Job 4:5–9)

I should tell you that Eliphaz, the first friend, claimed to have gotten his revelation from God. In the end, all three friends came to the same conclusion: Job's pain, loss, and suffering were the result of sin.

Our accusers aren't always our family or friends. We may be the ones blaming ourselves for our pain and suffering. Don't misunderstand me—I am speaking about myself, not Job, but in some instances my pain and suffering were the result of something I did or did not do.

Still, we can read Job's friends' reactions to his troubles in chapters 5 and 6. I do not understand why some people seem to believe that Christians do not suffer or endure sickness and loss. In Matthew, Jesus tells us that "in that way, you will be acting as true children of your Father in heaven. For he gives his sunlight to both the evil and the good, and he sends rain on the just and the unjust alike" (Matthew 5:45 NLT).

Job was able to hold his own with these friends because in Job 12:24–25, he expresses that no man or leader has real wisdom apart from God. God is superior and so is His wisdom. God is surprised by nothing we do or say. Job continues in chapter 13 by telling his friends they are like bad doctors who do not know what they are doing or talking about. Maybe some of their opinions were true, but they did not fit Job's situation. No, Job was not a sinless man. Romans 3:23 says we have all sinned and fall short of God's glorious standard. But Job was a righteous man, one who practiced obedience to God.

I don't know why God allows pain, but I do know that my pain has caused me to grow mentally and spiritually. It also causes me to depend more on the strength of God and less on myself. Pain can come in many forms, such as rejection, disappointment, and failure. The most important lesson I learned from Job is that God does not have to answer to anyone about what He does, says, or does not do. I also learned that God allows things to happen, and sometimes you and I will never know why. Maybe during those times, we need to think about the following verses:

"My thoughts are nothing like your thoughts," says the Lord. "And my ways are far beyond anything you could imagine. For just as the heavens are higher than the earth, so my ways are higher than your ways and my thoughts higher than your thoughts." (Isaiah 55:8–9 NLT)

Yet God has made everything beautiful for its own time. He has planted eternity in the human heart, but even so, people cannot see the whole scope of God's work from beginning to end. (Ecclesiastes 3:11 NLT)

Now let me bring this section to a close, but not before telling you what happened when God finally spoke. Job's friends wanted him to admit his sin and ask God for forgiveness. Job finally did just that, although not for the things they believed to be true. He asked forgiveness for secretly questioning God. He repented of his attitude and acknowledged God's great sovereignty and justice. Job's attitude came to light in chapter 37, when he began questioning God, and yet God remained silent. But in chapter 38, God challenged him about his attitude, asking a series of questions, including those listed below.

> Then the Lord answered Job out of the whirlwind, and said, Who is this that darkeneth counsel by words without knowledge? Gird up now thy loins like a man;

for I will demand of thee, and answer thou

me. Where wast thou when I laid the

foundations of the earth? declare, if thou hast

understanding. Who hath laid the measures

thereof, if thou knowest? or who hath

stretched the line upon it? Whereupon are the

foundations thereof fastened? or who laid the

corner stone thereof; When the morning stars

sang together, and all the sons of God shouted

for joy? Or who shut up the sea with doors,

when it brake forth, as if it had issued out of

the womb? When I made the cloud the

garment thereof, and thick darkness a

swaddling band for it, And brake up for it my

decreed place, and set bars and doors, And

said, Hitherto shalt thou come, but no further:

and here shall thy proud waves be stayed?

(Job 38:1–11 KJV)

Questioning Job as He did, God put Job in his place but also allowed him to see his mistake, for no man can know all of God's plans. God knew that Job, like us, could not answer His questions, but He asked them to allow Job to see firsthand how limited his knowledge was. Only through trusting in God can we hear what He is saying to us.

After God finished, Job did as we all should do—he humbled himself.

"I know that you can do anything, and no one can stop you. You asked, 'Who is this that questions my wisdom with such ignorance?' It is I—and I was talking about things I knew nothing about, things far too wonderful for me. You said, 'Listen and I will speak! I have some questions for you, and you must answer them.' I had only heard about you before, but now I have seen you with my own eyes." (Job 42:1–5 NLT)

At the end of Job's story, we read in Job 42:12–16 that he was consequently blessed by God. "The Lord blessed the latter part of Job's life more than the former part. He had fourteen thousand sheep, six thousand camels, a thousand yoke of oxen and a thousand donkeys. And he also had seven sons and three daughters. The first daughter he named Jemimah, the second Keziah, and the third Keren-Happuch. Nowhere in all the land were found women as beautiful as Job's daughters, and their father granted them an inheritance along with their brothers. After this, Job lived a hundred and forty years; he saw his children and their children to the fourth generation."

When reading Job, I have often wondered whether he had the same wife at the time when God restored him. I could not find any information saying she was not. Still, if you find yourself in a situation like Job's, please don't let the first thing that comes to your mind be "What did I do?" As Christians, we know when we are sinful because the Holy Spirit convicts our hearts. Try to resist self-pity because it can blind us from seeking help from the One who can answer all our questions.

God never told Job why he lost his children or his material possessions. He may not answer my questions or yours. But having God on my side is more important than trying to learn stuff I likely won't understand. God is in control of my life. If I keep my focus on Jesus Christ, I may have loss, pain, and suffering, but I'll also have hope. God is all-powerful, therefore I trust that He knows what He is doing in my life. I know without any doubt that God loves me. Whatever He does is in my best interest and for His glory.

Somewhat similar to Job, I lost all my memories and the ability to care for myself mentally, physically, or financially. I've had many dark and difficult days and nights, which I speak of openly and honestly in each of my books. But through it all, God has never failed me, nor has He forsaken me. At times, I've wondered where He was, but He gave me enough sense to know He was there and still is. Some who knew me before my illness may not agree with my next statement, but it is true.

As with Job, God has restored to me more than I had before and much more than I desire. He does not give because we deserve it. We deserve nothing. He gives and restores because of His love for us. This is another reason I am thankful that God has the last word about my life and my

situations. Many times, I gave up on myself. Because of my

illness, I was long ago counted out by most of you. But not

by God.

Chapter Seven: Handpicked by God

I have often heard people say that God does not work as He did in the days of the Bible. As a child of God, I choose to believe what is written in Malachi 3:6 (KJV): "For I am the Lord, I change not."

Therefore, choosing leaders for the people of God was never supposed to be left up to man. Throughout the Bible, I find God speaking directly to His servants and telling them the specific person He wanted to lead His people. A clear example of this can be found in 1 Samuel 16, when Samuel, a great prophet of God, was sent to the house of Jessie to anoint a new king. Samuel was the son of Elkanah and Hannah. His parents had given him back to God and placed him in the care of Eli, the high priest of the tabernacle at Shiloh. Samuel was called by God as a boy. He heard and responded as we all should: "Speak, your servant is listening" (1 Samuel 3:10 NLT).

In 1 Samuel 10, we find that Samuel had been given a mission: to annoint Saul as king.

Then Samuel took a flask of olive oil and poured it over Saul's head. He kissed Saul and said, "I am doing this because the Lord has appointed you to be the ruler over Israel, his special possession." (1 Samuel 10:1 NLT)

Later, after King Saul had rebelled against God, God told Samuel, "I am sorry that I ever made Saul king, for he has not been loyal to me and has refused to obey my command" (1 Samuel 15:11 NLT). God was not saying He made a mistake; He was expressing sorrow over Saul's disobedience and what Saul was doing to himself. Genesis 6:5–6 (NLT) shows a similar situation:

> The Lord observed the extent of human wickedness on the earth, and he saw that everything they thought or imagined was consistently and totally evil. So the Lord was sorry he had ever made them and put them on the earth. It broke his heart.

As a parent and grandparent I feel deep sorrow when my children are disobedient because I know from experience what the result will be. God loves us, and He had that same love for Saul. God did not change His mind about Saul. "He who is the Glory of Israel does not lie or change his mind; for he is not a human being, that he should change his mind" (1 Samuel 15:29).

Unfortunately, Saul had to pay for his sins, just as you and I do. His beginning was nothing like his end. Still, the Bible warns us that first impressions can deceive. Saul looked like the ideal king. He stood tall and strong, was courageous, and was good-looking to the human eye. In fact, the Bible says Saul was the most handsome man in Israel, standing a head taller than anyone else in the land (1 Samuel 9:2).

In 1 Samuel 9 it appears that Saul was humble. But as I continued reading, by the time I reached chapter 13, I came to the conclusion that his heart never belonged to God. Within it were jealousy, insecurity, arrogance, deceit, and impulsiveness. He did what he wanted the way he wanted so many times that God finally removed him as king.

"What have you done?" asked Samuel. Saul replied, "When I saw that the men were scattering, and that you did not come at the set time, and that the Philistines were assembling at Mikmash, I thought, 'Now the Philistines will come down against me at Gilgal, and I have not sought the Lord's favor.' So I felt compelled to offer the burnt offering." "You have done a foolish thing," Samuel said. "You have not kept the command the Lord your God gave you; if you had, he would have established your kingdom over Israel for all time. But now your kingdom will not endure; the Lord has sought out a man after his own heart and appointed him ruler of his people, because you have not kept the Lord's command." (1 Samuel 13:11–14)

Now let's go back to 1 Samuel 16 and the mission put before Samuel. I believe Samuel already knew what type of king he would anoint for God this time around. Although Saul had messed up, Samuel sought someone who had some of the same qualities and abilities as Saul but not his weaknesses. The only problem with this viewpoint is that it does not leave room for the fact that our weaknesses are what makes us useable to God.

I have come to realize that my strengths and abilities allow me to be useful to God. But I am also learning that my limitations and my lack of ability to do, think, write, or talk like a healthy person allows God to work through me for His glory.

We still make Samuel's mistakes today when looking for someone to fill an important position. People would compare the next king to the former king, Saul. But God had a way of selecting His next king, and it was not as Samuel would have thought. Samuel's lesson can teach us how God thinks in a situation like this.

First, God told Samuel where to find His next king and what to take with him on this journey. Second, in 1 Samuel 16, He instructed Samuel to fill his horn with olive oil and go to Bethlehem. Third, God told Samuel which house to go to: the house of Jessie. God was specific about the place and name. There may have been only one Jessie in this town, not like today. If there had been more than one, I believe God would have provided more details for clarity. Samuel also spoke of his fear of the task before him:

> But Samuel said, "How can I go? If Saul hears about it, he will kill me."
> The Lord said, "Take a heifer with you and say, 'I have come to sacrifice to the Lord.' Invite Jesse to the sacrifice, and I will show

you what to do. You are to anoint for me the one I indicate." (1 Samuel 16:2–3)

In my own experience of electing a new pastor, I've noticed that some church members are intimidated by those with authority, status, or money. Some refuse to vote, and others are easily influenced into voting the way others tell them. But here God calms Samuel's fears, enabling the prophet to do as he has been instructed. God will do the same for us when we face circumstances such as these.

When Samuel made it to Jessie's house, his next assignment was the purification rite for Jessie and his sons. When the sons entered, Samuel took a look at the oldest, Eliab, who was tall and handsome. Samuel thought he would the chosen one. Saul had fit that description too, and perhaps that is why Samuel thought Eliab would be the next king.

However, God corrects all misunderstanding. In the following passage, we see what He thought about Eliab and all Jessie's other sons:

But the Lord said to Samuel, "Do not look at his appearance or at his physical stature, because I have refused him. For the Lord does not see as man sees; for man looks at the outward appearance, but the Lord looks at the heart." So Jesse called Abinadab, and made him pass before Samuel. And he said, "Neither has the Lord chosen this one." Then Jesse made Shammah pass by. And he said, "Neither has the Lord chosen this one." Thus Jesse made seven of his sons pass before Samuel. And Samuel said to Jesse, "The Lord has not chosen these." (1 Samuel 16:7–10

NKJV)

Reading this closely, I came to the realization that God was telling me that my appearance does not reveal what type of person I am. For example, when people see me, they may see a well-dressed older woman who appears to have it all together. I walk the hospital halls, go in and out of the rooms of sick patients, and drive myself to and from destinations. And yet I am well aware that God carries me to and fro. Without Him, I couldn't even answer a simple question.

Looks can be misleading, which is one key reason individuals dealing with major depression can fool others about their health. The appearance does not always reveal what they are like, nor does it show others their true value or their feelings.

Only God knows what's in our hearts because He can see the inside as well as the outside of man. Eliab's true character is not revealed until 1 Samuel 17:28. We will talk more about him when we discuss David. Then we will see that he was critical and jealous of his youngest brother.

What if God had allowed Eliab to be king? We should be thankful that God knows our hearts, even if we are not always pleased with what's in them. Remember, through God, our hearts can be changed and renewed. "Therefore if any man be in Christ, he is a new creature: old things are passed away; behold, all things are become new" (2 Corinthians 5:17 KJV).

Finally, after receiving revelation from God that none of these sons were the future king, Samuel asked Jessie, "'Are these all the sons you have?' 'There is still the youngest,' Jessie replied. 'But he's out in the fields watching the sheep and goats.'" (1 Samuel 16:11 NLT).

David, the youngest son, was not important enough to this family to be invited to the first meeting with Samuel. If only they had known God's plans for David! If nothing else, the story of David should show us that man's opinion about us does not determine our future. It also has no control over our ending. David's family may have seen him as someone only worthy of caring for the flock, but God can turn a shepherd into a king and a deemed crazy person like myself into an author!

David Anointed King

Only after all the other sons were refused did Samuel learn of one other son—David. And if Samuel had not asked, he may never have learned that David existed. Samuel ordered Jessie to send for the boy at once.

So he sent for him and had him brought in. He

was glowing with health and had a fine

appearance and handsome features. Then the

Lord said, "Rise and anoint him; this is the

one." So Samuel took the horn of oil and

anointed him in the presence of his brothers,

and from that day on the Spirit of the Lord

came powerfully upon David. Samuel then

went to Ramah. (1 Samuel 16:12–13)

What did God have to say about this young man

whom He had chosen to be His future king?

"'He will do everything I want him to do.'" (Acts

13:22)

Yes, Samuel anointed David as king, but no one knew this except the ones present at the time of his anointing. He was not publicity anointed until much later because, legally, Saul was still king. During this time, God prepared David for his future responsibilities. God's plan for us may not have been revealed to others yet, but He is preparing us for that day and time, as He did for David.

"Then Judah's leaders came to David and crowned him king over the tribe of Judah" (2 Samuel 2:4). This event was similar to an inauguration of a public official already elected to office. And David had indeed been chosen by God for this office.

Being chosen by God does not mean man will accept us, as we can see in David's situation. Times were then as today; people decide who they think should be leaders or hold certain positions and how he/she should look. According to 2 Samuel 2, Judah remained loyal to David. But for seven and a half years, most of Israel refused to accept David as their king.

The Bible does not say David was chosen by God because he was perfect or would make a perfect king. It does, however, inform us of David's unfailing belief in God's faithfulness and forgiving nature. David's faith and trust in God's ability to protect is shown throughout his life.

For example, at a young age, he encountered Goliath. Goliath was said to be nine feet tall and wore a bronze helmet with a coat of mail that weighted 125 pounds. He was noted to have come from the giants the Israelites had been afraid of before they entered the Promised Land.

This giant had an armor bearer carrying a huge shield who walked ahead of him. But in the eyes of God, Goliath was no threat to the Israelites. God does not look at our appearance or size. Still, Saul had put a price on the giant's head, offering his daughter as a wife and exempting taxes for whoever killed him.

By this time David's three oldest brothers were enlisted in Saul's army to fight the Philistines. Saul had hired David to play music to calm the king's tormenting spirit. One day, when David was reporting for his duties with Saul and running errands for his father to his brothers on the battleground, he heard Goliath taunting the Israelites. As soon as the Israelites saw the giant, they ran in fear. David, on the hand, asked questions to learn whether what he was hearing was true. One question was, "What will a man get for killing this Philistine and ending his defiance of Israel? Who is this pagan Philistine anyway, that he is allowed to defy the armies of the living God?" (1 Samuel 17:26 NLT)

The other soldiers gaped in fear, including his brothers, who saw a giant. But David saw a sinful man challenging his God. As a young man, David saw that this was a situation for God. He had enough faith in God to know that something needed to be done about Goliath. And since the other men refused the challenge, David willingly stepped up, knowing he would not be in this fight alone because God would fight for him. David looked at the battle as you and I should look at ours: through the eyes of Jesus Christ. That way, we can fight more effectively.

In Ephesians chapter 6, the apostle Paul tells us to use every piece of the armor of God to resist and fight our enemies, so when the battle is finished we are still standing.

Stand firm then, with the belt of truth buckled around your waist, with the breastplate of righteousness in place, and with your feet fitted with the readiness that comes from the gospel of peace. In addition to all this, take up the shield of faith, with which you can extinguish all the flaming arrows of the evil

one. Take the helmet of salvation and the

sword of the Spirit, which is the word of God.

(Ephesians 6:14–17)

Although David did not have the Bible for

encouragement, he had faith in God. As onlookers criticized

and tried to discourage him, David took action, refusing to

accept his brothers' negative words.

But when David's oldest brother, Eliab, heard

David talking to the men, he was angry.

"What are you doing around here anyway?"

he demanded. "What about those few sheep

you're supposed to be taking care of? I know

about your pride and deceit. You just want to

see the battle!" (1 Samuel 17:28 NLT)

Eliab's words reveal the true nature of the man Samuel had believed to be the next king. This man was afraid to do anything about the situation but was willing to criticize David, his own brother, for doing what was right. "'Now what have I done?' said David. 'Can't I even speak?' He then turned away to someone else and brought up the same matter, and the men answered him as before." (1 Samuel 17:29–30)

Boldly David told Saul not to worry about a thing. He would fight the giant. But Saul, looking at David's size, age, and possibly even his shape compared to that of the giant, told David not to be ridiculous. There was no way he could go against this Philistine. He was just a shepherd boy, but Goliath had been in the army since he was a boy (1 Samuel 17:32–33 NLT).

I understand what Saul told David. Still, Saul does not appear to be in total disbelief of David's abilities as his brothers were. He simply looked at the situation through human eyes. David's faith in God allowed him to see the problem as a God problem. Therefore, the young boy and the older man saw the same situation with different outcomes. God had already proven Himself to faithful to David, which sealed his faith in God, as it should for us. Read what David told Saul in the next passage:

> But David said to Saul, "Your servant has been keeping his father's sheep. When a lion or a bear came and carried off a sheep from the flock, I went after it, struck it and rescued the sheep from its mouth. When it turned on me, I seized it by its hair, struck it and killed it. Your servant has killed both the lion and the bear; this uncircumcised Philistine will be like one of them, because he has defied the

armies of the living God. The Lord who

rescued me from the paw of the lion and the

paw of the bear will rescue me from the hand

of this Philistine." Saul said to David, "Go,

and the Lord be with you." (1 Samuel 17:34–

37)

Memory can be a powerful motivator. Remembering

God's faithfulness in our past reminds us of God's goodness,

power, and promises. David had not forgotten about the

times in the past that his God had rescued him.

After hearing David's words, Saul gave him

permission to fight the giant. He offered David his own

bronze helmet and coat of mail. But David was not familiar

with wearing battle gear, so after trying on the heavy items,

he took them off. As David made his move toward Goliath,

the giant got mad because his enemy had sent a boy do a

man's job—and an unarmed boy at that! In his madness, he
begins to scream at David.

> Meanwhile, the Philistine, with his shield
> bearer in front of him, kept coming closer to
> David. He looked David over and saw that he
> was little more than a boy, glowing with
> health and handsome, and he despised him.
> He said to David, "Am I a dog, that you come
> at me with sticks?" And the Philistine cursed
> David by his gods."(1 Samuel 17:41–43)

David confidently responded that the Lord would
defeat Goliath without the help of a sword, spear, or javelin.
"Today the Lord will conquer you, and I will kill you and cut
off your head. And then I will give the dead bodies of your
men to the birds and wild animals, and the whole world will

know that there is a God in Israel. And everyone assembled will know that the Lord rescues his people, but not with sword and spear. This is the Lord's battle, and he will give you to us." (1Samuel 17:46–47 NLT)

David moved toward Goliath in a fast run, a sling in his hand. The boy's first shot penetrated the giant in the forehead, the rock smashing into his head causing the giant to fall facedown onto the ground. David triumphed over the Philistine giant, and as he promised the giant, he "ran over and pulled Goliath's sword from his sheath. David used it to kill him and cut off his head." (1 Samuel 17:51 NLT)

Through all the talking and fighting, Saul did not even know who David was.

As Saul watched David going out to meet the Philistine, he said to Abner, commander of the army, "Abner, whose son is that young man?"

Abner replied, "As surely as you live, Your Majesty, I don't know." The king said, "Find out whose son this young man is." As soon as David returned from killing the Philistine, Abner took him and brought him before Saul, with David still holding the Philistine's head. "Whose son are you, young man?" Saul asked him. David said, "I am the son of your servant Jesse of Bethlehem." (1 Samuel 17:55–58)

I first found this hard to believe because I remembered Saul meeting David back in 1 Samuel 16:18–23, which says:

One of the servants answered, "I have seen a son of Jesse of Bethlehem who knows how to play the lyre. He is a brave man and a warrior.

He speaks well and is a fine-looking man.
And the Lord is with him." Then Saul sent
messengers to Jesse and said, "Send me your
son David, who is with the sheep." So Jesse
took a donkey loaded with bread, a skin of
wine and a young goat and sent them with his
son David to Saul. David came to Saul and
entered his service. Saul liked him very much,
and David became one of his armor-bearers.
Then Saul sent word to Jesse, saying, "Allow
David to remain in my service, for I am
pleased with him." Whenever the spirit from
God came upon Saul, David would take up his
lyre and play. Then relief would come to Saul;
he would feel better, and the evil spirit would
leave him.

But I failed to remember the circumstances in which they met: God had taken away His Spirit from Saul, and he was being tormented for his disobedience. With this thought in mind, I understood why he might not have recognized David. As you continue to read the life of David, you will see that Saul turned against him and tried to have him killed. Saul's attempts against David put in him in exile. He ran for his life, at times without needed supplies. David lived in caves in the wilderness, a price on his head by King Saul. But even when given the opportunity, David never laid a hand on Saul. However, the Bible says that Saul stopped trying to kill David only when David fled to Gath (1 Samuel chapters 19 through 27).

David's life story is among the most interesting in the Bible. However, my aim in this book is to show you that David, with all his sins, was still used by God. He never counted David out. For this, David never forgot to give God

His due credit. Read the book of Psalms, and you will find that starting in Psalm 2, David celebrates God's power. Psalms 3, 4, 5, and 6 speak of David's confidence and trust in God to protect and deliver him from his enemies and provide peace.

In Psalm 16, David offers the benefits of a relationship with God. Psalm 26 shows David declaring his loyalty to the one true God. David tells us in Psalm 27 that God is the answer for all of our fears, loneliness, rejection, uncertainty, sickness, and death. The psalmist says, "The Lord is my light and my salvation—so why should I be afraid?" (Psalm 27:1 NLT)

That said, David still was a sinner. He committed adultery with Bathsheba and arranged to have her husband, Uriah, killed. However, when confronted by the prophet Nathan for his sins, David didn't make excuses for himself as Saul had done when he spared the best of the Amalekite livestock against God's will (1 Samuel 15:3, 9). Nor did he do as I have done and, if truth be told, many of you have done. When confronted with his adultery and murder, David gave a simple, straightforward answer, just as ours should be. "I have sinned against the Lord" (2 Samuel 12:13 NLT). Mind you, he did not say he had sinned against Uriah, but God. Then Nathan replied, "Yes, but the Lord has forgiven you, and you won't die for this sin. Nevertheless, because you have shown utter contempt for the word of the Lord by doing this, your child will die" (2 Samuel 12:13–14 NLT).

During this event, David wrote Psalm 51, proving great insight into his character and offering hope for us. The life story of David allows us to see that, no matter how awful we may feel about our sins or what others may say or feel, we can go to God and seek His forgiveness and mercy, just as David often did.

Have mercy on me, O God, because of your

unfailing love. Because of your great

compassion, blot out the stain of my

sins. Wash me clean from my guilt. Purify me

from my sin. For I recognize my rebellion; it

haunts me day and night. Against you, and

you alone, have I sinned; I have done what is

evil in your sight. You will be proved right in

what you say, and your judgment against me

is just. For I was born a sinner—yes, from the

moment my mother conceived me. But you

desire honesty from the womb, teaching me

wisdom even there. Purify me from my sins,

and I will be clean; wash me, and I will be

whiter than snow. Oh, give me back my joy

again; you have broken me— now let me

rejoice. Don't keep looking at my

sins. Remove the stain of my guilt. Create in
me a clean heart, O God. Renew a loyal spirit
within me. Do not banish me from your
presence, and don't take your Holy Spirit from
me. Restore to me the joy of your
salvation, and make me willing to obey
you. Then I will teach your ways to rebels, and
they will return to you. Forgive me for
shedding blood, O God who saves; then I will
joyfully sing of your forgiveness. Unseal my
lips, O Lord, that my mouth may praise you.
(Psalm 51:1–15 NLT)

Imagine that a child of yours has done something so
bad that you are grievously hurt. What would happen if the
child opened his mouth and said what David said to God?

Thinking of this, I finally realized why God said that David was a man after His heart.

Just as in the case of David, God can and will forgive us, but He does not always erase the consequences of our sins. David's life and family were never the same as result of his sins (2 Samuel 12:1–23). After he was forgiven, David did not continue to dwell on his sins. He returned to God and started a new life (2 Samuel 12: 20–24).

David was a shepherd, poet, giant-killer, king, and ancestor of our Lord and Savior Jesus Christ. He had highs, failures, and deeply troubled times. But through it all, he never forgot God, and God never forgot him. David is considered one of the greatest men in the Old Testament, but along with his success are his sins. The Bible makes no effort to hide them from us, nor does it hide the fact of his repentance. Yet he was loved by God. Realizing how much I share in David's failures and not his greatness gives me hope.

David experienced joy for his forgiveness, even when he had to suffer the consequences of his sins.

At the beginning of David's story, it appears that he did not have much worth to those who should have loved him. But behind the scenes, you can see God working. This young man of little importance would one day become the greatest king of Israel, listed in the Hall of Faith in Hebrews chapter 11. I thank God for having the last word regarding my life, and you should too. David also offers an example through his prayer life. He did not count himself out, nor did he allow others to do so. He held on to his faith, showing us that he knew who would have the last word about his life and his salvation.

Chapter Eight: Counted Out by Religious Leaders

"They will never amount to anything in life." I can't count the times I heard this remark from older adults regarding our youth. On almost each occasion, I turn and say, "You think? That's the same thing you used to say about me." Their response: "Well, look at how they are dressed."

So I'm guessing some people think the way we dress determines our future. Maybe sometime in my past I had spoken these same words. Even if I did not say them out loud, I thought them. What about you?

Either way, I was wrong! So now I refuse to sit back silently if those words are spoken in my presence. Being inspired by God, I too will address some of these individuals as we glance at their lives.

It appears to me from studying the Word of God that there have always been some among us who think the love of God is only for the special few. If you and I are dealing with this issue, it's nothing new. But God's love and forgiveness were never just for the Jews and those who believed they were better than others. God is the creator of all, and He loves all. Counting people out and overlooking certain individuals has a long history. But when the ones with this attitude are also the ones God called to preach, then we have a problem that needs to be addressed.

Sinful People

I want to take a look at the prophet Jonah. Now, here was a man called by God. As part of his duties, he was sent to preach repentance to the people of Nineveh. According the Bible, Jonah hated the people of Nineveh and wanted vengeance not mercy. The Bible says that Nineveh was indeed a wicked city, but in the book of Jonah, God shows us that no one is above being saved by God if they repent. Jonah

responded to God by snubbing and indifference. He even ran

in the opposite direction than the way God told him to go.

Have you ever hated someone so badly that you did not want

God to save them?

I could not find evidence that Jonah and God had a

history. But I do believe that living during this era and being

a prophet, Jonah had to have known God. I think he would

have known this passage:

> If my people, who are called by my name, will
>
> humble themselves and pray and seek my face
>
> and turn from their wicked ways, then I will
>
> hear from heaven, and I will forgive their sin
>
> and will heal their land. (2 Chronicles 7:14)

The thought of these wicked people repenting and

receiving forgiveness did not bring Jonah any joy. He preferred that they would die and go to hell. In fact, he asked God to kill him instead of forcing him to preach to these people.

> This change of plans greatly upset Jonah, and he became very angry. So he complained to the Lord about it: "Didn't I say before I left home that you would do this, Lord? That is why I ran away to Tarshish! I knew that you are a merciful and compassionate God, slow to get angry and filled with unfailing love. You are eager to turn back from destroying people. Just kill me now, Lord! I'd rather be dead than alive if what I predicted will not happen." (Jonah 4:1–3 NLT)

Jonah's attitude toward this group of people is a prime example of the reluctance to treat others as they wish to be treated. I deal with this type of person almost every day. The individuals in Nineveh were labeled as pagans. To Jonah, this was the worst kind of human trash, not fit to live among good religious people. They were the untouchables, the overlooked. People who think like Jonah ask why God should take an interest in those types of people.

Does this sound like anyone you know? More importantly, which do you resemble more—Jonah or, like me, the untouchable? Either way, as a result of his feelings about these people, Jonah fled to Joppa and boarded a ship bound for Tarshish, which was in the opposite direction of Nineveh.

The book of Jonah teaches us that the people in Nineveh were wicked. Most of us have some knowledge of what this means, but Jonah does not tell us what their sins were. In the book of Nahum, I read more about their sins. Chapter 1 of Nahum offers us more insight into these people who are called Assyrians. First, they plotted against God. Second, they exploited the helpless. Third, they showed cruelty in war. Fourth, they practiced idolatry, prostitution, and witchcraft.

Although this book has only three chapters, it expresses precisely the sins Nineveh would be punished for if they did not repent. Still, Nahum tells us that "the Lord is slow to get angry, but His power is great, and He never let the guilty go unpunished." (Nahum 1:3 NLT)

Forgiven by God

Now that we have some sense of what going on, let's look at Jonah. He thought the Ninevites did not deserve to be saved because their sins were so great. Yet his sin of disobeying God was acceptable in his own eyes. But no sin gets a pass from God. In fact, Jonah's disobedience had deadly consequences for the lives of others.

Reading the book of Jonah, I realized the similarity between Jonah's sin and the sin of David in 1 Chronicles 21, which resulted in God punishing Israel for David's sins. Ezra, the noted author of 1 Chronicles, says David took a census of the Israelites. This by itself was not a sin, but David's reason for this census was wrong. David had allowed pride to enter his heart regarding his mighty army. That led him, as it has many of us, to forget the source of his real strength, which was God.

So David began to feel self-sufficient. Self-sufficiency takes us from God. God gave David the opportunity to choose the punishment. I don't know how often this happens, but this is what took place between and David and God: "So Gad went to David and said to him,

'This is what the Lord says: "Take your choice""" (1 Chronicles 21:11).

> And David said unto Gad, I am in a great strait: let me fall now into the hand of the Lord; for very great are his mercies: but let me not fall into the hand of man. So the Lord sent pestilence upon Israel: and there fell of Israel seventy thousand men. And God sent an angel unto Jerusalem to destroy it: and as he was destroying, the Lord beheld, and he repented him of the evil, and said to the angel that destroyed, It is enough, stay now thine hand. And the angel of the Lord stood by the threshing floor of Ornan the Jebusite. And David lifted up his eyes, and saw the angel of the Lord stand between the earth and the heaven, having a drawn sword in his hand stretched out over Jerusalem. Then David and the elders of

Israel, who were clothed in sackcloth, fell upon their faces. And David said unto God, Is it not I that commanded the people to be numbered? Even I it is that have sinned and done evil indeed, but as for these sheep, what have they done? let thine hand, I pray, O Lord my God, be on me, and on my father's house; but not on thy people, that they should be plagued. (1 Chronicles 21:13–17 KJV)

There are great parallels between the sins of David and Jonah. In my life, sin often has a domino effect. Dominos is the only game I can remember playing in my youth, so I get the comparison! Whenever I sin, a series of consequences always follows and can cause sorrow and suffering, as in the case of Jonah. For instance, tell one lie and you have to tell another to keep covering up for the first lie. Next thing you know, you're lying all over the place. Am I the only one this happens to?

Jonah's disobedience to God threatened the lives of the crew on the ship because God sent a storm. Now, the men on this ship had no clue what was going on. But Jonah knew. Jonah was asleep on the ship while the crew did all they could to save their lives. Finally, they asked Jonah who he was and where he came from. They also wanted to know his profession and nationality. The storm had gotten bad, so they were looking for answers.

> He answered, "I am a Hebrew and I worship the Lord, the God of heaven, who made the sea and the dry land." This terrified them and they asked, "What have you done?" (They knew he was running away from the Lord, because he had already told them so.) The sea was getting rougher and rougher. So they

asked him, "What should we do to you to make the sea calm down for us?"

"Pick me up and throw me into the sea," he replied, "and it will become calm. I know that it is my fault that this great storm has come upon you." Instead, the men did their best to row back to land. But they could not, for the sea grew even wilder than before. Then they cried out to the Lord, "Please, Lord, do not let us die for taking this man's life. Do not hold us accountable for killing an innocent man, for you, Lord, have done as you pleased." Then they took Jonah and threw him overboard, and the raging sea grew calm. At this the men greatly feared the Lord, and they offered a sacrifice to the Lord and made vows to him. Now the Lord provided a huge fish to swallow Jonah, and Jonah was in the belly of the fish three days and three nights. (Jonah 1:9–17)

Whether you believe this story or not is up to you. I believe every word of my Bible, and God told me to add this story for several reasons. First, we cannot run from God because there's no place for us to hide.

O Lord, you have examined my heart and know everything about me. You know when I sit down or stand up. You know my thoughts even when I'm far away. You see me when I travel and when I rest at home. You know everything I do. You know what I am going to say even before I say it, Lord. You go before me and follow me. You place your hand of blessing on my head. Such knowledge is too wonderful for me, too great for me to understand! I can never escape from your Spirit! I can never get away from your presence! If I go up to heaven, you are there; if I go down to the grave, you are there. If I ride the wings of the morning, if I dwell by the farthest oceans, even there your hand will guide me, and your strength will support me. I could ask the darkness to hide me and the light around me to become night—but even in darkness I cannot hide from you. To you the night shines as bright as day. Darkness and light are the same to you. (Psalm 139:1–12 NLT)

Second, God can use our mistakes to help the unsaved to come to know Him, just as He did with Jonah. For example, when Jonah stopped running and submitted to God, the storm calmed. The men on the ship saw this. Witnessing this mercy of God brought these men to faith and salvation.

Three, you may feel as I have (and as Jonah might have) that my past sins disqualify me from serving or being used by God. But read this passage and rejoice with thanksgiving, for we have a merciful God:

> Then the Lord spoke to Jonah a second time: "Get up and go to the great city of Nineveh, and deliver the message I have given you." This time Jonah obeyed the Lord's command and went to Nineveh, a city so large that it took three days to see it all. On the day Jonah entered the city, he shouted to the

crowds: "Forty days from now Nineveh will be destroyed!" The people of Nineveh believed God's message, and from the greatest to the least, they declared a fast and put on burlap to show their sorrow. When the king of Nineveh heard what Jonah was saying, he stepped down from his throne and took off his royal robes. He dressed himself in burlap and sat on a heap of ashes. Then the king and his nobles sent this decree throughout the city: "No one, not even the animals from your herds and flocks, may eat or drink anything at all. People and animals alike must wear garments of mourning, and everyone must pray earnestly to God. They must turn from their evil ways and stop all their violence. Who can tell? Perhaps even yet God will change his mind and hold back his fierce anger from destroying us." When God saw what they had done and how they had put a stop to their evil ways, he changed his mind and did not carry out the destruction he had threatened. (Jonah 3:1–10 NLT)

As you read the above passage, you may see as I do that these sinful individuals took action immediately. Not everyone does this, including myself. In reality, it takes some of us a little longer and a bit more convincing from God to get our attention. At least it did for me. However, the people in Nineveh, including the men on the ship, were ready and open to the word of God.

Not everyone you and I meet may be. I now know that at certain times in my life, I was not ready. But like these individuals, I too came to believe, and I repented. We must do more than just read the Word of God. To please Him, we must react in obedience to His Word.

Read all of Jonah and you will see as I do that God saved the people of Nineveh when they responded to Jonah's preaching. He will do the same for us. Our lives can be changed through Jesus Christ. None of us has the authority to count anyone out in this world. So, despite how others may feel about us or how we may feel about ourselves, God has plans for our lives. Ephesians 2:10 tells us, "For we are God's handiwork, created in Christ Jesus to do good works, which God prepared in advance for us to do."

The Life You Live

As the book of Jonah indicates, not only were the people in Nineveh saved but also the crew of the ship when they saw the actions of God. You and I are the hands and feet of Jesus Christ. Sometimes he uses our actions, words, and behavior to bring people to him. Just as God used the disobedience of a runaway preacher to change the lives of others, He is still able and willing to do the same with us.

This thought carried me back to Moses, who was by no means perfect. I speak of Moses in my previous books because God uses the life of Moses to help and encourage me in my struggles with mental illnesses. For this I am truly grateful.

Moses had a past, and through it he met the man who would become his father-in-law. In the book of Exodus chapter 2, Moses killed an Egyptian and buried him, believing no one saw him. He later learned that someone had seen him. (Someone always sees us.) So he ran.

I often hear on the news that people who committed crimes tried to escape punishment by running away. Some even fled their country. Well, they are not the first. Moses did the same thing long before Jesus Christ came and lived among us in a human form. Moses killed, he ran, and he ended up in a strange land, separated from family and friends. But finally, like me, he had to decide whether he trusted God more than he feared what a king could do to him.

I had to decide whether I trusted God more than I feared reactions to my mental illnesses once I opened up and wrote tell-all books. I know that, no matter how much faith Moses had or didn't have, this was not an easy decision for him. Moses had been humbled by his experience. Before the killing, he lived in the home of Pharaoh's daughter. But as a runaway killer, he learned the ways of the people he would one day lead. Read Exodus chapter 3 and allow God to show you how He prepared Moses for leadership.

"By faith [Moses] left Egypt, not fearing the king's anger; he persevered because he saw him who is invisible" (Hebrews 11:27). Moses may have felt alone and maybe even afraid, but he did not give up. When he arrived in Midian, he came to the aid of girls trying to get water for their flocks. For his help, he received an invitation to their home. He was more than happy to accept one in particular. This invitation resulted in a home and family for him because the patriarch gave Moses one of his daughters to marry. You can read this in Exodus 2:11–21.

It may appear that this section is about Moses. It could be, because at one time he had all the privileges of a grandson of Pharaoh, but he ended up in a bad situation. He could have given up on himself and been counted out by those who knew him, because now he was a fugitive. But most Bible readers know that God had plans for Moses. This was not his ending—it was his beginning. Surprising to some, Moses would become a great Jewish leader and set the exodus in motion. He ended up being the only prophet who spoke to God face-to-face as a man to his friend (Exodus 34:11). He was also a lawgiver and recorder of the Ten Commandments.

Nevertheless, this section is about the man who became Moses's father-in-law: Jethro—a Midianite also called Reuel, who originated from Midian son of Abraham.

I was inspired to add Jethro to this book for two reasons. First, God brings people in and out of our lives for different reasons. In the case of Moses and Jethro, both had something the other needed and God, the great planner, put them together. Moses needed shelter, love, friendship, a home, and the wisdom that he would gain from Jethro. Jethro

needed salvation, and through Moses, he would come to

know God. Jethro had some form of religious background

that prepared him to accept God when the opportunity arose.

This happened after Moses went back to free God's people

from slavery under the guidance of God.

So Moses went out to meet his father-in-law

and bowed down and kissed him. They

greeted each other and then went into the tent.

Moses told his father-in-law about everything

the Lord had done to Pharaoh and the

Egyptians for Israel's sake and about all the

hardships they had met along the way and

how the Lord had saved them. Jethro was

delighted to hear about all the good things the

Lord had done for Israel in rescuing them

from the hand of the Egyptians. He said,

"Praise be to the Lord, who rescued you from

the hand of the Egyptians and of Pharaoh, and

who rescued the people from the hand of the

Egyptians. Now I know that the Lord is

greater than all other gods, for he did this to

those who had treated Israel arrogantly." Then

Jethro, Moses's father-in-law, brought a burnt

offering and other sacrifices to God, and

Aaron came with all the elders of Israel to eat

a meal with Moses's father-in-law in the

presence of God. (Exodus 18:7–12)

Often those closest to us are the hardest to convince

about the greatness of God. Still, we can have an important

influence on those God places in our lives. This section is

also important because it shows that just as there was help for a runaway Moses in that day, God is still taking care of runaways today. God is still sending us people who need compassion, love, and mercy, no matter what they have done. In Moses's case, it wasn't over until God said it was.

Jethro was a priest, but he did not find or come to know the only true God until Moses came into his life. Moses was a great leader, and, under the guidance of God, he did great things.

Until God carried me back to read this book, I never thought about the importance of these two men's relationship. Nor had I realized how Moses, despite his sins, had found favor with God. The greatest gift you and I can offer another person is an introduction to God. The life of Moses inspired the life of Jethro. God had the last word in both lives.

Chapter Nine: Handpicked by Jesus Christ

Charles Swindoll said that anytime we engage in serious communication with another human being, especially someone deemed to be a lost case, we need to brace ourselves for a surprise. I must agree with this assumption. Do I have to say more? Look at my life. Who in their right mind would have thought I would become an author?

The worse the person appears to you, the greater the surprise. That's almost as interesting as watching God make a somebody out of a nobody. God has a way of turning people's lives around. This occurred numerous times in the Bible. It even happened to people who had been counted out by their community leaders.

Matthew

As Jesus was walking along, he saw a man named Matthew sitting at his tax collector's booth. "Follow me and be my disciple," Jesus said to him. So Matthew got up and followed him. Later, Matthew invited Jesus and his disciples to his home as dinner guests, along with many tax collectors and other disreputable sinners. But when the Pharisees saw this, they asked his disciples, "Why does your teacher eat with such scum?" When Jesus heard this, he said, "Healthy people don't need a doctor—sick people do." (Matthew 9:9–12 NLT)

In the above passage, the religious leaders called Matthew scum. I have called people worse. At times, I have thought worse about myself. Have you? Believe it or not, we didn't invent the act of judging and labeling people. This started long before any of us were born. But that does not give us the right to do so.

But what is scum? Well, I'm glad you asked! *Merriam-Webster's Collegiate Dictionary* says that a scum is a low, vile, or worthless person or group of people. Can you imagine that someone man views as a worthless lowlife can be valuable to God? If not, you may need to take a close look at Matthew.

We meet my next subject, Matthew, in Capernaum, working as a tax collector in a tax booth. (We find his location in Mark 2:13–17.) Matthew's original was name Levi, and he had more to lose financially than any of the other disciples, but he also had much more to gain. Still, as a tax collector for the Roman government, he was hated and viewed as a traitor by his fellow Jews.

Matthew collected taxes from citizens and business owners. Jewish people believed tax collectors informed the Roman government about their finances, so they viewed them as traitors and thieves. Many people today hate tax collectors, and this story gave me insight into the origins of this hatred and bitterness.

In Matthew's day, tax collectors were to take a commission on the taxes they collected, but most of them overcharged and kept the profits. The profits gained from their job gave them a different status than the people they collected from. Matthew had a well-paying job although he was viewed as a lowlife. Still, he had friends within his own circle, probably fellow tax collectors. I would guess some of these friends may also have changed after their encounter with Jesus at this dinner.

As a tax collector, Matthew had to be good with numbers, an insightful bookkeeper, and a keen observer of his environment. God does not need to add anything to our skills because He has already given us all we need. Therefore, when He calls us, He just allows us to take the skills we were using for Satan and now use them in a way that brings Him glory.

I see this in Matthew. When Jesus asked him to follow him, Matthew got right up and left. I read nowhere in the Bible that he hesitated in any way. I read nothing about him having faith in Jesus before they met. He apparently had not heard about Jesus before this night.

No, when he met Jesus for himself and accepted the calling, his heart began the process of changing. He left all he had, including the lifestyle he had gotten used to. Through Jesus Christ, Matthew was given a new life and a new name. For a despised tax collector, this had to have been an amazing experience. Imagine a hated tax collector suddenly belonging to the Son of God and being accepted by the most important "Person" in the world.

The talent he brought from his past was his ability to use his pen. The gospel that bears his name came as the result of accepting Jesus Christ as his Lord and Savior. Through the life of Matthew, we can see that we are a work in progress and that God has given each person skills and abilities to use for Him. Whenever we begin to trust God fully with what He has given us, we'll find a new life.

Matthew couldn't have known that God would one day take the skills he used to cheat and steal from people and instead use those talents to record the life story of the greatest person who ever lived. God could do this because He knows our beginning, our end, and everything in between. He is in control of our future.

Matthew wrote his gospel to his fellow Jews to prove

that Jesus Christ is the Messiah and to explain God's kingdom. So in the first chapter, we find a complete genealogy of Jesus Christ. Matthew moves on and tells of Jesus's birth and early childhood, including his family's escape to Egypt and their return to Nazareth.

According to Matthew, the people of Israel were waiting and looking for a Messiah who would deliver them from Roman oppression. But Matthew's book shows that God did not send Jesus to be an earthly king but a heavenly king with a lasting kingship. Jesus came to die for all people to save us from our sins, not to save us from one another or from other races. Matthew provides firsthand accounts of his life with Jesus, connecting the Old and New Testaments. He showed us that Jesus Christ fulfilled prophecy, as we see in Matthew 5:17 (NLT): "Don't misunderstand why I have come. I did not come to abolish the law of Moses or the writings of the prophets. No, I came to accomplish their purpose."

Matthew, the scum, became one of the twelve disciples of Jesus Christ, trusted by God to write about our Lord and Savior. As such, Jesus was with Matthew and the other disciples physically until he ascended into heaven and then spirituality through the Holy Spirit (Acts 1:4). Because of the resurrection of Jesus Christ, the Holy Spirit will always be with us as long as we are here. He will never leave us, just as Jesus promised the disciples: "But the Comforter, which is the Holy Ghost, whom the Father will send in my name, he shall teach you all things, and bring all things to your remembrance, whatsoever I have said unto you" (John 14:26 KJV).

Another Tax Collector

I wish to speak of another tax collector before we

leave this section. This came to mind recently as I was speaking to a fellow volunteer. This particular volunteer had just purchased one of my earlier books. Knowing how busy he was, I asked him if he'd had time to start reading.

"Yes, and it's interesting."

"In what way?" I asked.

"It made me think about writing my own book."

"Everyone has a book within them. If I can write, then anyone can, through the grace of God," I told him, trying to encourage him.

But then he said, "I would write about how hated I am because I am short."

I must say I did not see this coming. All I could say was, "Man, who hates you?"

He said to me, "Short people are hated all over the world. I know this because I have traveled all over."

I didn't know what to say. This was an older African

American man who should, at his age, be enjoying some level of joy and peace. But here he was, confessing to me the pain he had always endured because of his height.

I finally said to him, "Some of our most powerful people were not tall. Look at Martin Luther King. He was not so tall. And we have no idea how tall our Lord and Savior Jesus Christ was!"

As he talked, my mind shifted to my first grandson, who must have taken after me and his mother because he is so short. In fact, he may be the shortest grandchild among my seven, although he is the oldest. He is the shortest among all the boys on both sides of his family. I have witnessed the look of pain that shoots across his face at family gatherings when he is called short. I cringe with him when one of the taller family members pulls his head under their arm and rubs his head, especially when it's someone his age.

I have seen his expression when others in our family

downplay someone's importance because he/she is short. I began to wonder just how hated my own grandchild may feel because of his height. Was he going to be like this man I was speaking to—one day old and talking of being hated all his life because of his height? Earlier, I spoke about the power of our words and the fact that they can build up or tear down a person's self-worth. Now, if you are reading this and you are a grandparent, you will understand when I say I was deeply saddened by these thoughts.

I must admit that my sadness quickly turned to joy, because I know God loves all of us. My prayer is that my grandson would one day come to this same awareness of being loved and valued by God. But I also thought of Zacchaeus, the short tax collector noted in the Bible. The Bible tells us this man's height, but it tells us nothing about the height our Lord and Savior. In my opinion, this is so no one will feel left out. He is the height and size of all of his followers, whether we are short, medium, or tall in stature.

Now let's get to Zacchaeus's story. Jesus was on his way to Jerusalem for the last time. By this stage in his ministry, Jesus had a large following. He had performed many miracles, including a few I noted in this book—for instance, raising his friend Lazarus from the dead. So the people were rushing to get a close look at Jesus. One of the individuals in this crowd was a man named Zacchaeus. But he was too short to see over or through this crowd, so he ran ahead and climbed up a sycamore tree beside the road and waited for Jesus to pass by.

This often happens to me at the movies. I pick a seat with a perfect view, then a tall person sits in front of me on both sides. No matter how I move in my seat, I cannot see a thing. But there is no tree to climb, even if I could.

Zacchaeus was not just a tax collector; he was a chief tax collector. This may have meant he had others working under him or for him. The book of Luke may be the only place he is mentioned, but the story of Zacchaeus has the potential to influence and change the lives of many individuals. The Roman government recruited Jews to spy on their own people and report back about their earnings. To finance their great world empire, the Roman government put heavy taxes on everyone under their control. This is just one of the reasons tax collectors were called traitors and other ugly names, and it's why they were unpopular. The more money these tax collectors were able to take from their fellow Jews, the more they had for themselves. Zacchaeus, a Jew by birth, chose to work against his people, who were oppressed by the Roman government.

So we have a disliked and despised short tax collector in a crowd trying to see Jesus. I doubt there was anyone in this group who was willing to help Zacchaeus to the front of the crowd or pick him up so he could look over the crowd.

But whether anyone helped him or not, he seemed highly motivated to see Jesus. This may explain John 6:44 (NLT): "For no one can come to me unless the Father who sent me draws them to me, and at the last day I will raise them up."

This story reminds me of the woman with the issue of blood. There were many people in this crowd. I'm not sure whether Zacchaeus was the only short man there that day, but he is the only one Jesus looked at and called by name. "'Zacchaeus!' he said. 'Quick, come down! I must be a guest in your home today'" (Luke 19:5 NLT). I read nothing that indicates they had met before, but Jesus knew his name.

This confirms our importance to Jesus. So does Psalm 139:13 (NLT): "You made all the delicate, inner parts of my body and knit me together in my mother's womb." Also, John 10:3 (NLT) says "The gatekeeper opens the gate for him, and the sheep recognize his voice and come to him. He calls his own sheep by name and leads them out." Jesus knows our names, and he care for us. We are important to God.

So you and I need to do as Zacchaeus and be willing to act when Jesus calls our name. "Zacchaeus quickly climbed down and took Jesus to his house in great excitement and joy" (Luke 19:6 NLT). The people in this crowd who thought they knew Zacchaeus's ending were displeased about Jesus's concern for him. "'He has gone to be the guest of a notorious sinner,' they grumbled." (Luke 19:7 NLT) The onlookers had the same complaint about Matthew, who became one of Jesus's twelve disciples and the author of the book of Matthew.

Still, Zacchaeus was not put off by their words. He focused instead on the fact that he was a sinner in need of a savior.

But Zacchaeus stood up and said to the Lord,

"Look, Lord! Here and now I give half of my possessions to the poor, and if I have cheated anybody out of anything, I will pay back four times the amount." (Luke 19:8)

Realizing he needed to change his life, Zacchaeus gave to the poor and made restitution with substantial interest. This proves his heart was changed.

Jesus responded, "Salvation has come to this home today, for this man has shown himself to be a true son of Abraham. For the Son of Man came to seek and save those who are lost." (Luke 19:9–10 NLT)

Onlookers may not have wanted to hear that the man they hated so was a true son of Abraham. But we are not saved by our family names and traditions. Nor are we condemned for our bad pasts. Jesus shows that our faith is more important than our family name. Jesus came to save all who are lost. No matter our size, height, or appearance, our past, or our previous way of life, we are all important to God.

Chapter Ten: The Apostle Paul

Aside from Jesus, no one shaped the history of Christianity more than Saul. His name would later change to Paul, and he was probably counted out by all Christians in his day. And understandably so. He started off a strong believer in getting rid of everyone who confessed faith in Jesus Christ. Before moving forward, though, let's take a few minutes to look at Saul's beginning. He was born in Tarsus, from the tribe of Benjamin with Hebrew ancestry. King Saul, Israel's first king, came from this tribe (Philippians 3:1–5; Samuel 10:20–24)

Saul's ancestors were Pharisees, devoted to the Law of Moses. They did not want their children to be contaminated by Gentiles. Saul became an expert in Jewish history after studying under the rabbi Gamaliel. From this, he became a lawyer (expert in Jewish law). He later became zealous in his own faith, which did not seemed to allow for compromise. Apparently, his faith and teaching did, however, allow for the hatred and despising of Jesus Christ.

We meet Saul for the first time at the stoning death of Stephen. Stephen was one of the seven leaders chosen to supervise food distribution to the needy in the early church. "His accusers took off their coats and laid them at the feet of a young man named Saul" (Acts 8:58 NLT). Before his death, Stephen asked God not to charge the stoners for their sins (Acts 7:60) This would include Saul, who assisting in his death by holding the coats of Stephen's killers.

I often tell my grandchildren that if they are present at a crime and don't run for their life or speak up against whatever is going on, then they are a part of that crime. The Bible says nothing about Saul trying in any way to stop the stoning of Stephen. Saul likely knew that Stephen was a man of God, since the Bible says, "Stephen, a man full of God's grace and power, performed amazing miracles and signs among the people" (Acts 6:8 NLT).

Nevertheless, the killing of Stephen had the opposite effect than intended. Instead of stopping the growth of Christianity, the faith expanded. In fact, the persecution of Christians forced them out of Jerusalem into Judea and Samaria, fulfilling the second part of Jesus's command: "But you will receive power when the Holy Spirit comes on you; and you will be my witnesses in Jerusalem, and in all Judea and Samaria, and to the ends of the earth" (Acts 1:8). Stephen's death helped the church obey Christ's final command to take the gospel worldwide.

I find the life of Paul captivating for three reasons: his frantic persecution of Christians, his great transformation, and the way God changed his life. Every time I study Paul, I think of my own conversion and how God got my attention. So in the following section, I will compare my experience to

Paul's.

Paul was so zealous in his hostility toward Christianity that it became personal. He went from door to door, dragging Christians from their homes and placing them in prison. His goal was to destroy the early church of God and stop the spreading of the good news about Jesus Christ.

Eventually, he got so mad and so eager to destroy the followers of God that he obtained permission from the Jewish leaders to travel to Damascus to bring Christians back to Jerusalem to be punished. This was a 150-mile journey for Paul, but he was determined to bring men and women back to Jerusalem in chains (Acts 9:1–2).

As he moved forward on his mission, his whole life changed without warning. Everything he lived for was gone. Has God ever done this to you? Things are going well when, without warning, the phone rings at an odd hour. Or you go the doctor for a routine checkup and find yourself in shock.

What did the doctor say? "Did you say what I think you said?"

Maybe it sometimes takes something like what Paul was about to go through in order to get our attention. Your life is forever changed from that day forward. Oh, let me tell you—just as with Paul, God reached down and got my attention one day. Nobody can get our attention like God. It's astonishing how quickly our minds turn back to who is actually in control.

Like Paul, I used to think I had control over my life. But also like Paul, God brought me to my knees. I eventually gained some level of sense to know who was in control. I don't have to tell that it was not me.

Although there are still gaps in my memories, I know I had an independent and proud spirit. I know this because God has revealed to me the trouble it had caused in my past. And I believe that same proud spirit contributed to the downfall of Saul but also the introduction of Paul. He went

on this mission with a made-up, one-sided mind about what

would take place once he arrived. But he completely

underestimated the power of God.

> As he neared Damascus on his journey,
>
> suddenly a light from heaven flashed around
>
> him. He fell to the ground and heard a voice
>
> say to him, "Saul, Saul, why do you persecute
>
> me?" "Who are you, Lord?" Saul asked. "I am
>
> Jesus, whom you are persecuting," he replied.
>
> "Now get up and go into the city, and you will
>
> be told what you must do." The men traveling
>
> with Saul stood there speechless; they heard
>
> the sound but did not see anyone. Saul got up
>
> from the ground, but when he opened his eyes

he could see nothing. So they led him by the
hand into Damascus. (Acts 9:3–8)

Paul later refers to the above experience as the start of
his new life in Jesus Christ. This experience forced Paul to
acknowledge Jesus as Lord, confess his own sins, give his
life to Christ, and resolve to obey Him. At the center of this
life-changing experience, he saw Jesus Christ—not in a
vision but the risen Christ Himself. During this whole
process, God made sure Paul was taken care of and also gave
him back his sight:

Then Ananias went to the house and entered
it. Placing his hands on Saul, he said, "Brother
Saul, the Lord—Jesus, who appeared to you
on the road as you were coming here—has
sent me so that you may see again and be

filled with the Holy Spirit." Immediately, something like scales fell from Saul's eyes, and he could see again. He got up and was baptized. (Acts 9:17–18)

My life-changing experience happened in a mental institution, when I answered the call of Jesus Christ. I don't remember seeing a face, but I will always remember the love and warmth I felt coming from the place where He had placed my attention. I can still feel the arm reaching out and pulling me from the hole of impending death to everlasting life. My personal encounter with Jesus changed my life as it did with Paul. I lost my cognitive capability for years and still need assistance of others. I could see but needed help to express what I was seeing. But through it all, God took care and is still taking good care of me.

Paul never lost this fanatical drive, but from that point

on, he used it to spread the gospel. He now had a relationship with Jesus Christ, the man he once hated. Paul thought he was pursuing heretics and blasphemers because Jesus did not conform to Paul's expectations of what and who the Messiah should be. *Heresy* is defined by *Merriam-Webster's Collegiate Dictionary* as an opinion or doctrine contrary to church dogma. *Blasphemy* is defined as the act of insulting or showing contempt or lack of reverence for God. Jesus wanted Paul to know, just as he tells us, that worshiping him is not heresy. Anyone who persecutes the children of God is also guilty of persecuting Jesus Christ. Believers are the body of Jesus Christ on earth. Jesus says that on Judgment Day, all will be brought before God, and He will separate them into two groups—those favored and those cursed—based on how they treated Jesus's followers.

"The King will reply, 'I tell you the truth, when you

did it to one of the least of these brothers and sisters, you were doing it to me.' . . . And he will answer, 'I tell you the truth, when you refused to help the least of these my brothers and sisters, you were refusing to help me.'" (Matthew 25:40, 45 NLT)

Biblical scholars suggest that Paul relied on his own traditional understanding and assumed that Jesus's claims were false; therefore, he thought they were a threat to the religious establishment (Philippians 3:6). But then, after his encounter with Jesus Christ, Paul was a different person. But many did not believe in his change.

Saul spent several days with the disciples in Damascus. At once he began to preach in the synagogues that Jesus is the Son of God. All those who heard him were astonished and asked, "Isn't he the man who raised havoc in Jerusalem among those who call on this name? And hasn't he come here to take them as prisoners to the chief priests?" Yet Saul grew more and more powerful and baffled the Jews living in Damascus by proving that Jesus is the Messiah. (Acts 9:19–22)

Paul's faith in Jesus Christ would be tested many times, but it also came with great blessing that changed the lives of many individuals. Still, as in that day, it is difficult to change a reputation. We can understand why Paul would have a hard time getting Christians to believe in him. But in 2 Corinthians 10:1–11 (ESV), Paul defends his ministry.

I, Paul, myself entreat you, by the meekness and gentleness of Christ—I who am humble when face to face with you, but bold toward you when I am away!— I beg of you that when I am present I may not have to show boldness with such confidence as I count on showing against some who suspect us of walking according to the flesh. For though we walk in the flesh, we are not waging war according to the flesh. For the weapons of our warfare are not of the flesh but have divine power to destroy strongholds. We destroy arguments and every lofty opinion raised against the knowledge of God, and take every thought captive to obey Christ, being ready to punish every disobedience, when your obedience is complete. Look at what is before your eyes. If anyone is confident that he is Christ's, let him remind himself that just as he is Christ's, so also are we. For even if I boast a little too much of our authority, which the Lord gave for building you up and not for destroying you, I will not be ashamed. I do not want to appear to be frightening you with my letters. For they say, "His letters are weighty and strong, but his bodily presence is weak, and his speech of no account." Let such a person understand that what we say by letter when absent, we do when present.

By this time, Saul was called Paul. His ministry required purpose, patience, and discipline. Living as a Christian takes hard work, self-denial, and the training found in the Word of God. Until the conversion of Paul, little had been done to take the gospel to non-Jews. Paul worked hard, trying to convince Jews that the Gentiles were as important as the Jews and were acceptable to God. In Acts 28:28 (NLT), Paul said, "So I want you to know that this salvation from God has also been offered to the Gentiles, and they will accept it."

In Philippians chapter 3, we see his humility as he tells us that the Bible is our safeguard, both morally and theologically. Paul had impressive credentials and the right upbringing, nationality, family background, and inheritance. Yet he said all he accomplished in life was worthless compared with the greatness of knowing Christ. He gave up everything—family, friends, and freedom—to know Christ and his resurrection power.

But whatever were gains to me I now consider loss for the sake of Christ. What is more, I consider everything a loss because of the surpassing worth of knowing Christ Jesus my Lord, for whose sake I have lost all things. I consider them garbage, that I may gain Christ and be found in him, not having a righteousness of my own that comes from the law, but that which is through faith in Christ—the righteousness that comes from God on the basis of faith. I want to know Christ—yes, to know the power of his resurrection and participation in his sufferings, becoming like him in his death, and so, somehow, attaining to the resurrection from the dead. (Philippians 3:7–11)

My wish is that you would read the whole story of this man. If you already have, then do it again, as I did for this book. Then take a close look at a man who, by all accounts, would have been counted out. Yet God said no; Paul would not be counted out by man.

From the life of Paul I learned that God can save whomever He wants: the good, the decent, the wicked, and those we say are evil. Watching the news daily, I hear about people committing crimes similar to those committed by Paul. We may believe such individuals are unworthy of redemption. Well, so were you and I. If we look at our lives, we might be tempted to say we haven't done what they did. But we've had the same thoughts. Yet we somehow think we are better.

Because of Jesus Christ, we all have the potential for change. Paul never gave up.

"I served the Lord with great humility and with tears and in the midst of severe testing by the plots of my Jewish opponents. You know that I have not hesitated to preach anything that would be helpful to you but have taught you publicly and from house to house. I have declared to both Jews and Greeks that they must turn to God in repentance and have faith in our Lord Jesus. And now, compelled by the Spirit, I am going to Jerusalem, not knowing what will happen to me there. I only know that in every city the Holy Spirit warns me that prison and hardships are facing me. However, I consider my life worth nothing to me; my only aim is to finish the race and complete the task the Lord Jesus has given me—the task of testifying to the good news of God's grace." (Acts 20:19–24)

Paul kept his focus on his message of salvation, and

he never missed an opportunity to share the good news about

Jesus Christ. Paul was satisfied with whatever he had,

wherever he was, as long as he could do the work of God.

God took him from being a persecutor of Christians to a

preacher for Jesus Christ (Acts chapter 20). In Philippians

chapter 1, Paul shows that, even in prison, he had no

bitterness. He felt only joy for being called to preach the

good news about Jesus Christ.

And I want you to know, my dear brothers and

sisters, that everything that has happened to

me here has helped to spread the Good News.

For everyone here, including the whole palace

guard, knows that I am in chains because of

Christ. And because of my imprisonment,

most of the believers here have gained

confidence and boldly speak God's message

without fear. (Philippians 1:12–14 NLT)

I will leave Paul with messages he gave to his

beloved son in Christ—Timothy. He told Timothy never to

forget that Jesus Christ was born a man into King David's

family and that he was raised from the dead. This was the

good news Paul preached. And because he didn't waver from

this message, he suffered and was put in chains like a

criminal. But the word of God could not be chained (2

Timothy 2:8–9 NLT).

Finally, note what Paul says in Philippians 3:12–14:

Not that I have already obtained all this, or

have already arrived at my goal, but I press on

to take hold of that for which Christ Jesus

took hold of me. Brothers and sisters, I do not

consider myself yet to have taken hold of it.
But one thing I do: Forgetting what is behind
and straining toward what is ahead, I press on
toward the goal to win the prize for which
God has called me heavenward in Christ
Jesus.

Paul goal was to keep his focus on Jesus Christ, a mission he never forgot after his first encounter with Jesus Christ. Paul, like me, had things in his past that he would probably have liked to forget. In my case, God fixed this problem by taking away my memories, both the good and the bad. Still, I have done things since that I am ashamed of. For many years, I've wondered what all I did and said in my past. But also like Paul, because of my hope in Jesus Christ, I can let go of any past guilt and look forward to what God will help me to become.

If you still hold on to the past, let it go. Realize that you are forgiven, and move on to a life of faith. Don't hold your past over your head, and don't allow others to use it to count you out. It is not over for you until God says it is over! That's good news, people!

Chapter Eleven: Jesus Christ, Chosen by God

At first, I did not understand why God impressed on me to choose this person to focus on in this chapter. I could not see how we could regard Jesus as counted out. But then, through the Holy Spirit, I realized that the most important person who ever walked this earth was counted out by many people including, regrettably, me.

Everyone has a personal definition of what it means to be rejected or disqualified. In my opinion, people are rejected and disqualified when they are overlooked because of who they are, where they came from, and their past, status, lack of education, disabilities, or heredity. Second, individuals are rejected or disqualified when they are misjudged or underestimated, and when others fail to realize who they really are. Third, individuals who should be a part of our lives are rejected when we purposely leave them out of our lives. We do not make time for these individuals, nor do we want to make time. Fourth, when we do not believe the things a person says, thinking that he/she may be crazy, and we don't want them in our lives.

That said, from the beginning of his life on earth, our Lord and Savior Jesus Christ was counted out, starting with his own brothers and people in his hometown. But don't be quick to judge because by the time I am done with this section, you may find as I did that we are no different from those we judge. Jesus tells us in John 15:18 (NLT), "If the world hates you, remember that it hated me first." Despite all Jesus Christ did for this world, he was hated and rejected by many in his day and still today.

As we look at the individuals noted in this book, I want you to examine your relationship with Jesus to ensure that you are not still counting him out of your life. I will be the first to admit that, at one time in my life, I rejected Jesus by counting him out of my daily life. I was a church member then, and if someone had asked me if this was true, I would have said no! And most likely I would have gotten mad that you had the nerve to ask me this question. But now I know better. I thank God that I can admit this and can move on because I have been forgiven for this foolish mistake.

Let's take a look at Jesus. He came on the scene in an unexpectedly humble beginning. Many people knew the Messiah was coming. I don't know what was in the minds of the people in that day, but Jesus was not what they thought he should have been. In fact, according to Matthew, many Jews thought that the expected Messiah was going to be a military and political deliverer.

Because of God's word through Micah, many people believed the Messiah would be born in Bethlehem.

"But you, Bethlehem Ephrathah, though you

are small among the clans of Judah,

out of you will come for me one who will be

ruler over Israel, whose origins are from of

old, from ancient times." (Micah 5:2)

God used Micah to reveal the birthplace of His Son

hundreds of years before Jesus was born. Jesus would be the

promised eternal king in the line of David, who would come

to earth and live as a man. Chapter 5 of Micah gives the

clearest Old Testament prophecies of the coming of Jesus

Christ. It seemed the believers of that day did not expect a

king to come as a suffering servant, although the prophet

Isaiah says he would.

Who hath believed our report? and to whom is

the arm of the Lord revealed?

For he shall grow up before him as a tender plant, and as a root out of a dry ground: he hath no form nor comeliness; and when we shall see him, there is no beauty that we should desire him. He is despised and rejected of men; a man of sorrows, and acquainted with grief: and we hid as it were our faces from him; he was despised, and we esteemed him not. Surely he hath borne our griefs, and carried our sorrows: yet we did esteem him stricken, smitten of God, and afflicted.

But he was wounded for our transgressions; he was bruised for our iniquities: the chastisement of our peace was upon him; and with his stripes we are healed.

All we like sheep have gone astray; we have turned every one to his own way; and the Lord hath laid on him the iniquity of us all. He was

oppressed, and he was afflicted, yet he opened

not his mouth: he is brought as a lamb to the

slaughter, and as a sheep before her shearers is

dumb, so he openeth not his mouth. (Isaiah

53:1–7 KJV)

Some of the Jews did not believe that a king would

come with such humble beginnings in a place they did not

like. But according to the books of Mark and Matthew, Jesus

did. Mark says that Jesus grew up in Nazareth. Both disciples

say that Jesus's hometown of Nazareth was a small town

between the Sea of Galilee and the Mediterranean. The city

was despised and avoided by many Jews because of its

reputation of independence. Nazareth was a crossroads for

the trade route; therefore, people living here would come in

contact with many other cultures. In addition, because of the trade business and people coming in and out, world news reached them quickly. (Matthew 2 and Mark 1). God sent His Messiah from Nazareth, which was unthinkable, unbelievable, and surprising to some. I concluded this from some conversations in the Bible.

When Jesus had finished these parables, he moved on from there. Coming to his hometown, he began teaching the people in their synagogue, and they were amazed. "Where did this man get this wisdom and these miraculous powers?" they asked. "Isn't this the carpenter's son? Isn't his mother's name Mary, and aren't his brothers James, Joseph, Simon and Judas? Aren't all his sisters with us? Where then did this man get all these things?" And they took offense at him. But

Jesus said to them, "A prophet is not without honor except in his own town and in his own home." And he did not do many miracles there because of their lack of faith. (Matthew 13:53–58)

Now let's look at John chapter 1. Jesus had met Philip, and Philip went looking for Nathanael and told him about Jesus. He said he had met the very person Moses and the prophets wrote about: Jesus, the son of Joseph from Nazareth. Nathanael asked what others must have been thinking: "Can anything good come from Nazareth?" (John 1:46 NLT)

Philip told Nathanael to come see for himself, so this is what he did. Then he became one of Jesus's disciples. It was a good thing he was willing to meet Jesus for himself rather than hold back because of his prejudiced views about the Messiah—where he was to come from, and from what family. This is a great lesson for us! Nathanael's outspoken opinion about Jesus resulted in Jesus calling him an honest man, because he knows the hearts of all individuals (John 1:47–50).

Through Jesus Christ, we can learn true humility.

Though he was God, he did not think of equality with God as something to cling to. Instead, he gave up his divine privileges; he took the humble position of a slave and was born as a human being. When he appeared in human form, he humbled himself in obedience to God and died a criminal's death on a cross. (Philippians 2:6–8 NLT)

Can you imagine living in richness with your Father

in heaven, and giving it all up to be poor? Revelation 21:15–18 tells us that the walls of the heavenly kingdom are made of jasper and the city with pure gold, with gates of pearls. But God's love for us was so strong that gave His only-begotten Son for our sins (John 3:16).

> The Word became flesh and made his
> dwelling among us. We have seen his glory,
> the glory of the one and only Son, who came
> from the Father, full of grace and truth. (John
> 1:14)

When Jesus was born, God became a man. So Jesus was 100 percent man and 100 percent God, completely human and completely divine.

The Son is the image of the invisible God, the firstborn over all creation. For in him all things were created: things in heaven and on earth, visible and invisible, whether thrones or powers or rulers or authorities; all things have been created through him and for him. He is before all things, and in him all things hold together. (Colossians 1:15–17)

Jesus understood the rumors about his identity. I think this may be why he asked his disciples, "Who do people say that the Son of Man is? (Matthew 16:13 NLT)

After the disciples responded, Jesus asked them who they said he was. God revealed to Peter who Jesus was, so he answered, "You are the Messiah, the Son of the living God" (Matthew 16:16 NLT). Still, the people did not expect their Messiah to be a restorer, bringing people back from the dead, but he could and he did.

Jesus knew firsthand what it felt like to live with rejection. He was rejected even in his hometown. so noted in Luke 4:

> And he said unto them, Ye will surely say unto
> me this proverb, Physician, heal thyself:
> whatsoever we have heard done in Capernaum,
> do also here in thy country.
> And he said, Verily I say unto you, No prophet
> is accepted in his own country. (Luke 4:23-24
> KJV)

If rejection and rumors are painful to us, they had to be even more painful for the sinless Jesus Christ. Jesus was rejected by the Jews because, in their eyes, he failed to do what they expected. Our expectations of people can mess us up. Many of the Jews assumed their Messiah would release them from the oppression of the Roman government. They thought he would establish an eternal kingdom with Israel as the leading nation in the world because he was believed to be Messiah spoken of by Moses.

In other words, the people of Jerusalem believed Jesus had come to deliver them (Matthew 21). In reality, Jesus did come to deliver them, but not the way they hoped. What he had to offer was much better than what they wanted. People could not believe the true reason Jesus came to this earth, which was to seek and save those who are lost (Luke 19:10). Nonetheless, he was accused and rejected by his own family and the teachers of the law. In Mark 3, after hearing him speak, his family believed Jesus was crazy:

Then Jesus entered a house, and again a crowd gathered, so that he and his disciples were not even able to eat. When his family heard about this, they went to take charge of him, for they said, "He is out of his mind." And the teachers of the law who came down from Jerusalem said, "He is possessed by Beelzebul! By the prince of demons he is driving out demons." (Mark 3:20–22)

Not only was Jesus rejected, he was also deserted by many of his followers because of his message (Matthew 26:55–56).

Aware that his disciples were grumbling about this, Jesus said to them, "Does this offend you? Then what if you see the Son of Man ascend to where he was before! The Spirit gives life; the flesh counts for nothing. The

words I have spoken to you—they are full of
the Spirit and life. Yet there are some of you
who do not believe." For Jesus had known
from the beginning which of them did not
believe and who would betray him. He went
on to say, "This is why I told you that no one
can come to me unless the Father has enabled
them." From this time many of his disciples
turned back and no longer followed him.
(John 6:61–66)

Not all his disciples left him at this point; some
abandoned him later. Studying the life of Jesus with his
disciples, I came across something I had not noticed before.
If you read Matthew 10 and look down at the listing of the
disciples, you will see as I did that Judas, his betrayer, is at
the bottom of the list. In Mark chapter 3 and in Luke chapter

6, Judas is listed last as well.

I don't know if this is because Judas was the last disciple to be selected or if it was because he had no real relationship with Jesus. I found only two instances of communication between Jesus and Judas. In John 12, Mary anointed Jesus's feet with a twelve-ounce jar of expensive perfume. "But Judas Iscariot, the disciple who would soon betray him, said, 'That perfume was worth a year's wages. It should have been sold and the money given to the poor'" (John 12:4–5 NLT).

But John goes on and tells us, "Not that he cared about the poor—he was a thief, and since he was in charge of the disciples' money, he often stole some for himself" (John 12:6 NLT). Yet, this statement by Jesus expresses his opinion about these events and the importance of Mary's offering: "'Leave her alone,' Jesus replied. 'It was intended that she should save this perfume for the day of my burial'" (John

12:7).

The second instance of Jesus interacting with Judas is found in Matthew 26:20–25:

When evening came, Jesus was reclining at the table with the Twelve. And while they were eating, he said, "Truly I tell you, one of you will betray me." They were very sad and began to say to him one after the other, "Surely you don't mean me, Lord?" Jesus replied, "The one who has dipped his hand into the bowl with me will betray me. The Son of Man will go just as it is written about him. But woe to that man who betrays the Son of Man! It would be better for him if he had not been born." Then Judas, the one who would betray him, said, "Surely you don't mean me, Rabbi?" Jesus answered, "You have said so."

After the episode with Mary and the perfume, Judas realized that Jesus was not going to start a political rebellion to overthrow the Roman government. But if you look at Mark 10:35–40 (KJV), Judas did not appear to be the only disciple who held this view.

And James and John, the sons of Zebedee, come unto him, saying, Master, we would that thou shouldest do for us whatsoever we shall desire. And he said unto them, What would ye that I should do for you? They said unto him, Grant unto us that we may sit, one on thy right hand, and the other on thy left hand, in thy glory. But Jesus said unto them, Ye know not what ye ask: can ye drink of the cup that I

drink of? and be baptized with the baptism

that I am baptized with?

And they said unto him, We can. And Jesus

said unto them, Ye shall indeed drink of the

cup that I drink of; and with the baptism that I

am baptized withal shall ye be baptized: But to

sit on my right hand and on my left hand is

not mine to give; but it shall be given to them

for whom it is prepared.

Judas may have not been the only disciple who had the wrong beliefs regarding Jesus's true reasons for coming to this earth. However, we do know he was the one who went to the leading priests and asked, "How much will you pay me to betray Jesus to you?" (Matthew 26:15 NLT). Judas is the man described in Psalm 41:9 (NLT), which says, "Even my best friend, the one I trusted completely, the one who shared

my food, has turned against me."

In John 13, we see Jesus's love for his disciples,

including his betrayer:

When he had finished washing their feet, he

put on his clothes and returned to his place.

"Do you understand what I have done for

you?" he asked them. "You call me 'Teacher'

and 'Lord,' and rightly so, for that is what I

am. Now that I, your Lord and Teacher, have

washed your feet, you also should wash one

another's feet. I have set you an example that

you should do as I have done for you. Very

truly I tell you, no servant is greater than his

master, nor is a messenger greater than the

one who sent him. Now that you know these

things, you will be blessed if you do them. I
am not referring to all of you; I know those I
have chosen. But this is to fulfill this passage
of Scripture: 'He who shared my bread has
turned against me.' I am telling you now
before it happens, so that when it does happen
you will believe that I am who I am. Very
truly I tell you, whoever accepts anyone I send
accepts me; and whoever accepts me accepts
the one who sent me." (John 13:12–20)

Jesus also faced being denied by Peter, one who never
failed to follow him throughout Jesus's ministry. Yet, after
the arrest of Jesus Christ, Peter denied him three times:

Now Peter was sitting out in the courtyard,
and a servant girl came to him. "You also

were with Jesus of Galilee," she said. But he

denied it before them all. "I don't know what

you're talking about," he said. Then he went

out to the gateway, where another servant girl

saw him and said to the people there, "This

fellow was with Jesus of Nazareth." He denied

it again, with an oath: "I don't know the

man!" After a little while, those standing there

went up to Peter and said, "Surely you are one

of them; your accent gives you away." Then

he began to call down curses, and he swore to

them, "I don't know the man!" Immediately a

rooster crowed. (Matthew 26:69–74)

Why did the man whom Jesus called the Rock deny

Jesus? Out of fear. And because he was human, not perfect.

Jesus was not looking for perfection, because he knew no one was perfect. Jesus's greatest desire, then and now, are people who are willing to be changed by his love.

Despite his failures and denial of Jesus, Peter went on to do great things for God, including being the first great voice of the gospel during and after Pentecost (Acts 2). Jesus knew who his betrayer was, just as he knows about us. He knew Peter would deny him, and he knows what you and I will do that will also hurt him. Yet he loves us unconditionally and will forgive us whenever we ask. The difference between Peter and Judas was that Peter believed God would forgive him despite his failures. I don't think Judas made it to this point of belief.

Jesus Christ is the walking example of God's love for us. No one expected Jesus to get arrested and die on the cross, but he did. All those involved with his crucifixion, including the soldiers who gambled with his clothes, counted him out. Let's not forget Satan, who misunderstood the death of Jesus. The Bible says in Luke 22:3 that Satan entered into Judas Iscariot. Satan may have believed that using Judas would end God's plans to save mankind. But Judas and all the others, including the brothers of Jesus who rejected his message, did not believe in his true identity. Jesus's death and resurrection were the most important parts of the plan of God (Luke 22).

In John 2:19 (NLT), Jesus told the Jews, "Destroy this temple, and in three days I will raise it up." But no one expected him to rise from the dead—certainly not Thomas.

So the other disciples told him, "We have seen the Lord!" But [Thomas] said to them, "Unless I see the nail marks in his hands and put my finger where the nails were, and put my hand into his side, I will not believe." A week later his disciples were in the house again, and Thomas was with them. Though the doors were locked, Jesus came and stood among them and said, "Peace be with you!" Then he said to Thomas, "Put your finger here; see my hands. Reach out your hand and put it into my side. Stop doubting and believe." Thomas said to him, "My Lord and my God!" Then Jesus told him, "Because you have seen me, you have believed; blessed are those who have not seen and yet have believed." (John 20:25–29)

Jesus's resurrection is the foundation of the Christian faith. Luke 24 tells us that because Jesus rose from the dead, we can see the immense power of God over life and death. Also, as believers, we know we are headed for redemption. We now know that death has not conquered, and we too will rise from the dead and live forever with Jesus Christ. The resurrection of our Lord and Savior was the beginning of Christianity. And Jesus was seen by many after his resurrection, as Paul states in 1 Corinthians 15:3–9:

> For what I received I passed on to you as of first importance: that Christ died for our sins according to the Scriptures, that he was buried, that he was raised on the third day according to the Scriptures, and that he appeared to Cephas, and then to the Twelve. After that, he appeared to more than five hundred of the brothers and sisters at the same time, most of whom are still living, though some have fallen asleep. Then he appeared to James, then to all the apostles, and last of all he appeared to me also, as to one abnormally

born. For I am the least of the apostles and do
not even deserve to be called an apostle,
because I persecuted the church of God.

Jesus's brothers lived with him, and they underestimated his true identity. His disciples also lived with him, and they too misjudged the power he applied to their situations. In fact, after his resurrection, the disciples remembered things he had told them, and they came to believe Jesus and the Scriptures (John 1:22). Religious leaders in Jesus's day knew what the Old Testament said about Jesus, but they refused to accept him as the Son of God. In John 5:39–40 (NLT), Jesus told them, "You search the Scriptures because you think they give you eternal life. But the Scriptures point to me! Yet you refuse to come to me to receive this life."

God paid a high price, the life of His Son, for our

sins. Jesus Christ forgives our sins and cancels our punishment, so who should we listen to? Jesus crossed all barriers so we could live. He did not come to take away our challenges but to change us on the inside. A change that is so powerful, it allows and empowers us to deal with our problems through the perspective of his Father.

At times, I have misjudged and overlooked the power of Jesus to handle situations, sickness, or trials in my life. What does this say about me? It accurately answers the question I put to each of you at the beginning of this section. What does it say about you? Keep this in mind: our belief and faith in Jesus Christ made us right with God (Romans 9:30).

Jesus did not disown or desert Peter or Paul. Peter started out with Jesus, but later he denied knowing him. Paul started out trying to destroy and kill his believers. Jesus Christ had great plans for these individuals. He has plans for us too. It is not over until God says it is. So don't let anyone count you out, and just as important—don't count yourself out.

Final Thoughts: God's Plans for Me

I learned about one of the plans God has for me about a month ago. Believe me when say it was an amazing surprise. Is this not what God does best? Here I was in Mississippi, trying to finish my third book. I had just gotten a call from my baby sister, Janet, who recently got stationed in Seattle, Washington. She told me she has joined a church.

Now, see how our God works. She somehow ended up on the committee that plans the church conferences. In the meeting with the other committee members, she didn't want to say much because she's new in this town and church. Although she has traveled all over the world through the military, God put her there for a reason. Her job was part of His plans for her.

Anyone who has joined a new organization will understand how she feels. But during the meeting, the First

Lady of this church announced that they needed another speaker at the conference. She asked if any of them knew of a speaker they could get.

She looked at each member, then her gaze fell on my sister. The Holy Spirit spoke my name loudly in Janet's spirit. She opened her mouth in obedience and said, "I have a sister in Mississippi who just finished writing her second book and is working on her third. Maybe she would come."

The First Lady asked the title of my second book. Janet said, "*What Do You Have That God Can Use: A Book of Faith*."

It turned out that the name of the conference was "What Do You Have That God Can Use?"

Two days later, I agreed to go, and they agreed to take care of me. But I was uneasy while we were making the plans for this trip. I still have problems speaking, and I also have problems reading and following instructions. In the midst of crowds, I can get confused.

This won't be my first time to fly from Mississippi, but it will be the first time I've done it alone. As a child of God, I'm never alone, so this feeling is not going to hold me back.

I also had to deal with telling people about this blessing. Believe me, this blessing came only through the working of my God. Yet, the only way you will know how He works is by reading His Word and stepping out in faith and having a relationship with Him. And through this relationship, memories are made. I previously wrote that remembering can be a powerful tool. I could look back and know that God is doing everything necessary to sustain and keep me—not just to function but to truly live. Nevertheless, I have received many positive and negative responses regarding my books.

Still, I told no one how I felt about the pending

speaking event. Thank God for knowing our inner concerns, feelings, and doubts.

Then someone said to me, " I would hate to have to speak after Tasha Cobbs, because she is so good." Up to this point, I hadn't thought a lot about how unimportant and unequipped I was compared to the others I would share the stage with. I pray that comment was not intended to hurt my feelings, but it put my focus back on my limitations. I was bothered by these words, but I never considered backing out. Deep in my spirit, my trust of God is deeply embedded.

I began to move through my days with some level of confidence, not in myself but in the God who had gotten me to this point in my life. God opened this door and knows my weaknesses and my strengths. Who knew who would be on that stage, but I know my self-worth, my value, and my importance to Him. And like any loving parent, He was not sending me out by myself. He knows that the Holy Spirit would be with me and speak on His behalf through me.

With these thoughts, my mind was at rest, but God did not stop there. He wanted to give me more comfort with His love. One day as I was making my bed, He said, "I want you to enjoy this period in your life. Ever since you were five, your mind has been filled with other people's problems and responsibilities. The average person has never had to deal or live with these duties. I know what you are feeling now, but I want you to listen.

"Craig and Vanity spent Easter Sunday with you, and they both gave you a list of what they wanted you and Kent to cook. Vanity wanted a coconut pie and Craig wanted banana pudding. Think about this: you had more Easter dinner guests than just the two of them, so the desserts ended up being shared by others. However, Craig and Vanity knew these were their desserts because you had made them just for them.

"On that stage at the conference, I want you to know that I put this event together just for you. Tasha Cobbs will share the stage with you; you won't share the stage with her because you will be the main attraction!"

But there is room on "my" stage for everyone. Do you understand? God knows just how and when to make His children feel important because to Him we are "somebody special."

Another thing I love about God is His capability to meet me at my own level of understanding. The example God gave me was real for me, and I immediately understood what He was saying. Thus, my answer to God was yes. From that day forward, I have been working to finish my book and planning for my trip. A trip planned by God and for God. I will be there to represent my Lord and Savior Jesus Christ, and God will be glorified.

By the time this book is in print, this event will be

over, but others will follow. I will tell you more about this particular conference in my next book. Oh, my God, there's going to be another book!

I ask for your continued prayers as I move forward with my eyes on Jesus Christ. And I will do the same for each of you. I don't know His plans for us, but I know that as long as He is the One making the plans, you and I will be better than okay.

With every breath and step I take, God shows me that it is not over until He says it is. Sometimes we may believe we are at the end of our rope, or we have taken all we can take. But because of Jesus Christ, we are never at the end of hope.

> That is why we never give up. Though our
> bodies are dying, our spirits are being renewed
> every day. For our present troubles are small

and won't last very long. Yet they produce for

us a glory that vastly outweighs them and will

last forever! So we don't look at the troubles

we can see now; rather, we fix our gaze on

things that cannot be seen. For the things we

see now will soon be gone, but the things we

cannot see will last forever. (2 Corinthians

4:16–18 NLT)

I know from firsthand experience that it is much

easier to give up than it is to fight. We all face many

problems that make us think about giving up, but we must

not let them diminish our faith in God. Second Corinthians

4:8–11 (NLT) says:

We are pressed on every side by troubles, but

we are not crushed. We are perplexed, but not

driven to despair. We are hunted down, but never abandoned by God. We get knocked down, but we are not destroyed. Through suffering, our bodies continue to share in the death of Jesus so that the life of Jesus may also be seen in our bodies. Yes, we live under constant danger of death because we serve Jesus, so that the life of Jesus will be evident in our dying bodies.

I pray that if this not true for you, then after reading this book, it will be. It is not over until God says it is. This is nothing less than God's amazing grace. To God be the glory.

Looking Ahead

When God gave me the title, I knew why this book may be the most important of the three books I've written. Individuals who are counted out or overlooked in our society need to know that allowing others to determine our futures may be our greatest mistake. God specializes in doing the impossible for those of us who are counted out. That way, He can get the glory from our lives. If we allow God, He will bring about the opportunity for us to have the last word—not with hate but with love and humility.

www.ingramcontent.com/pod-product-compliance
Lightning Source LLC
Chambersburg PA
CBHW062149080426
42734CB00010B/1625